Religion and Education

Religion and Education

The Forgotten Dimensions of Religious Education?

Edited by

Gert Biesta and Patricia Hannam

BRILL

SENSE

LEIDEN | BOSTON

Cover illustration: Photograph by Steve Deeming

All chapters in this book have undergone peer review.

The Library of Congress Cataloging-in-Publication Data is available online at http://catalog.loc.gov

Typeface for the Latin, Greek, and Cyrillic scripts: "Brill". See and download: brill.com/brill-typeface.

ISBN 978-90-04-44637-3 (paperback)
ISBN 978-90-04-44638-0 (hardback)
ISBN 978-90-04-44639-7 (e-book)

Printed by Printforce, the Netherlands

Advance Praise for
Religion and Education: The Forgotten Dimensions of Religious Education?

"Following the publication of the Commission on Religious Education (CoRE) Final report there has been a mood change in the theoretical discussions about the nature and purpose of RE. The true game-changing significance of the Commission's introduction of the language of worldview is beginning to dawn. This fine collection of essays from a variety of talented thinkers represents some green shoots heralding the paradigm shift that might be to come. The authors are a mixture of well-known old hands, including three who served as commissioners on the CoRE team, and some mid-career rising stars whose ideas will no doubt become increasingly influential. Their interests are wide-ranging across, amongst others, the representation of Islam, the nature of religion and of education, the place of theology in Catholic schools, GCSE question setting, pedagogy and hermeneutics. But the common theme is the offer of an alternative to a lazy approach to notions like knowledge, understanding and academic rigour that forget that our pupils are developing human beings and not just consumers of knowledge organisers. This book is a must-read for anyone wanting to grapple with the future direction of a Religious Education that takes seriously both religion and education."
– **Trevor Cooling, Professor, National Institute for Christian Education Research, Canterbury Christ Church University, UK**

"This compilation is a valuable contribution to all people interested in religion and worldviews in public education. It can be seen as a call for focus on the fundamentals of religion in education. The volume comprises of several independent scholarly essays on what is the very 'soul' of religion in public education: religion and education. Each internationally recognized author draws from his or her scholarly background in their contribution so that the reader will find the issues brought up to resonate with and be relevant to several disciplines. While the individual works are diverse in their approach, topics and execution, the editorship and authors have managed to produce a contribution with coherence and high-quality. We simply need this kind of critical scholarship to lay the foundation against which more peripheral, but also important, issues can be analysed and solved, but also, when necessary, kept in the periphery of what is called good research, curriculum or practice concerning religion and worldviews in education. To me this book represents an urgent call for focus. Policy-makers, scholars, teachers and students alike will find this com-

pilation a versatile, timely and high-quality research-based contribution to the discussion on religion in public education."
– **Martin Ubani, Professor of Religious Education, University of Eastern Finland**

"Religious education is more important now than ever before as children and young people grow up in an increasingly diverse and complex world. This text nourishes – *educare* – and leads us – *educere* – into a broader and more ambitious understanding of religious education. The emphasis on the relational nature of the subject and a clarion call for a reframing and recontextualization of the subject rooted in both education theory and new understandings of 'religion' will no doubt bring the reader to attention and action. In their different ways, the authors challenge and disrupt some of the current understandings of religious education presenting their wisdom with depth, discernment and insight. This is an exciting contribution in current debates about the subject."
– **Kathryn Wright, CEO, Culham St Gabriel's Trust**

Contents

Acknowledgements

We would like to express our gratitude to the Culham St Gabriel's Trust for providing us with the funding for the seminar upon which this book is based. We are also very grateful to the authors of this book – for their willingness to share their thoughts and ideas and for their patience and good spirit during the editing process. Finally, we would like to thank John Bennett, our editor at Brill | Sense, for his support in bringing this project to fruition.

Notes on Contributors

David Aldridge

is Reader and Director of Research in the Education Department at Brunel University London. He is co-editor of the *British Educational Research Journal* and assistant editor of the *Journal of Philosophy of Education*. His publications on the philosophy of religious education include numerous journal articles and chapters and the monograph *A Hermeneutics of Religious Education*, for Bloomsbury.

Gert Biesta

is Professor of Public Education in the Centre for Public Education and Pedagogy at Maynooth University, Ireland, and Professorial Fellow in Educational Theory and Pedagogy at the Moray House School of Education and Sport, University of Edinburgh, UK. He has worked at a number of universities in the UK and continental Europe. He has degrees in education (Leiden University, the Netherlands) and philosophy (Erasmus University, the Netherlands) and obtained his PhD from Leiden University in 1992. His interest in education was triggered when he worked in medical education. His interest in religion dates back from his time as a student of theology – a study that was interrupted due to a car accident. He writes about educational theory and policy and the theory and philosophy of educational and social research. His work has appeared in twenty different languages. Recent books include *The Rediscovery of Teaching* (Routledge, 2017); *Obstinate Education: Reconnecting School and Society* (Brill | Sense, 2019); and *Educational Research: An Unorthodox Introduction* (Bloomsbury, 2020). He serves as co-editor of the *British Educational Research Journal* and associate editor of *Educational Theory*.

Robert A. Bowie

holds a Chair in Religion and Worldviews Education at Canterbury Christ Church University, UK, where he is also Director of the National Institute for Christian Education Research, a research centre specialising in research in Christian Worldview Education. He is Executive Chair of the Association of University Lecturers in Religion and Education and a National Teaching Fellow of Advance Higher Education. He is a former secondary school teacher, with experience in Catholic schooling in England and schools in Turkey and Japan. An educator of RE teachers for ten years, and author of multiple school textbooks in ethics, he now leads research in Religious Education, Christian Education and aspects of ethics and values in professional practice. He has written extensively on teaching with sacred texts and hermeneutics, British values in education, and dignity and human rights education, the subject of his PhD. His spiritual formation owes much to the Jesuit Catholic state school in London where he was a pupil, and the ecumenical and international Taizé community founded by Roger Schütz, which he returns to whenever he can. He is married with two children and lives in the Weald of Kent, in south-east England.

Denise Cush

is Emeritus Professor of Religion and Education at Bath Spa University, UK. The first female Professor of RE in the UK in 2003, she was a member of the Commission on Religious Education 2017–2018, and Deputy Editor of the *British Journal of Religious Education* from 2011–2018. She has an MA in Theology from Oxford University, an MA in Religious Studies from the University of Lancaster, a PhD in Religious Education from the University of Warwick, and in 2016 she was awarded an Honorary Doctorate from the University of Uppsala, Sweden. Her interests include Buddhism, Hinduism, Christianity and alternative spiritualities such as Paganism, as well as religious education. She taught Study of Religions and Religious Education at school and university levels and also trained teachers of religious education, both primary and secondary. Publications include *Buddhism,* a still much-used textbook for A level (Hodder, 1994), co-editing the Routledge *Encyclopaedia of Hinduism* (2008), editing *Celebrating Planet Earth, a Pagan/Christian Conversation* (Moon, 2015) and many other publications on RE, Buddhism and Paganism. Her most recent publication is "Religion and Worldviews in Education" in *Education Studies: A Student Guide* (edited by C. A. Simon & S. Ward; 4th ed., RoutledgeFalmer, 2019).

Patricia Hannam

has been County Inspector/Adviser for Religious Education, History and Philosophy for Hampshire County Council, UK since 2009. With varied education experience in and out of the classroom, her research interests lie in the art of teaching and putting education theory into practice through curriculum formation and a commitment to education that ensures the conditions for life. Her publications in the field of education include articles and chapters in various books and journals. Her research monograph *Religious Education and the Public Sphere* was published by Routledge in 2018.

Ruth Heilbronn

researches and lectures at UCL Institute of Education, where she has led various teams engaged in teacher education. She previously taught in inner London secondary schools and worked as an LEA advisor. She has written on the epistemology of practice, mentoring, practical judgement and ethical teacher education. John Dewey has figured largely in her work, as an editor of several collections and organiser of conferences. She is an executive member of the Philosophy of Education Society of Great Britain. In 2018 she co-edited *Dewey and Education in the 21st Century: Fighting Back* (Emerald Publishing), together with Christine Doddington and Rupert Higham.

David Lewin

is Senior Lecturer in Philosophy of Education at the University of Strathclyde. His research interests include philosophy of education, philosophy of religion, and philosophy of technology. David has published numerous articles and chapters on such interdisciplinary notions as 'Silence and Attention', 'The Pharmacological nature of Educational Technology,' and 'Post-secularism' as well as on figures such as Meister Eckhart, Martin Heidegger, Pierre Teilhard de Chardin, and Paul Ricoeur. David is sole author of two books: *Technology and the Philosophy of Religion* (Cambridge Scholars, 2011) and *Educational Philosophy for a Post-secular Age* (Routledge, 2016). David's current research focuses on notions of didactical and pedagogical representation and reduction. He co-leads the 'Experiments in Educational Theory' research group based at the University of Strathclyde (www.exet.org).

Joyce Miller

was an Associate Fellow in the Religions and Education Research Unit at the University of Warwick (WRERU). In 2007 she retired as Head of Diversity and Cohesion at Education Bradford, prior to which she was a senior lecturer in religious studies at the University of Wolverhampton, where she specialised in initial teacher training. She taught in secondary schools in Coventry and Northumberland. She was a member of the Commission on RE (2016–2018), and of the advisory group on *A New Settlement for RE* set up by Charles Clarke and Linda Woodhead. She is a former Chair of the RE Council, AREIAC, Bradford SACRE and the Schools Linking Network. She led the first phase of the REC's work on Learning Outside the Classroom and she chaired the monitoring and evaluation groups of *REsilience* and the RE Quality Mark. She co-ordinated the enquiry on Community Relations and RE for the APPG on RE (2014). She has lectured and written widely on RE especially in relation to community cohesion and extremism. In 2014 she co-edited *Religion in Education: Innovation in International Research* (Routledge) and she is a former editor of *REsource,* the journal of the Professional Council for RE.

Farid Panjwani

is Associate Professor at the Institute of Education, University College London, where he is also the founding Director of the Centre for the Study of Education in Muslim Contexts (CEMC). Dr. Panjwani received his doctorate from University of Oxford in philosophy of education. He also holds a master's degree in Education and International Development from the University of London and a degree in Business Administration. With his broad interest in various fields of the humanities, Dr. Panjwani has researched, taught and published on several topics including religious education in schools, inter and intra-religious diversity, interface between religious and citizenship education, place of imagination in learning and the rise of extremisms in contemporary times. He has acted as a consultant to many organisations, both nationally and internationally. He was a member of the National Commission on Religious Education which published its final report last year.

Lynn Revell

is a reader in religion and education at Canterbury Christ Church University, UK, where she has worked on the PGCE for Religious Education and Citizenship, and now leads the Doctorate in Education. She has worked in secondary schools as a teacher of Religious Education and for the Commission for Racial Equality. Lynn is currently involved in research on looking at the significance of extremism in education and free speech in schools and FE. She has published work on the representation of Islam in RE, and the impact of the requirement to promote 'fundamental British values' in schools and colleges.

Catherine Robinson

has a BA (Hons) in Religious Studies from Stirling University and a PhD in Religious Studies from Lancaster University. She taught at Bath Spa University for nearly 30 years where her main interests included issues of gender and sexuality in religions and Indian religions (especially Hinduism and Sikhism) in the modern period. She was also a member of the local SACRE and the regional steering group of Learn, Teach, Lead RE. Together with Denise Cush, she worked on the Living Religion: Facilitating Fieldwork Placements in Theology and Religious Studies project that received the Shap Award for 2013 for its contribution to the field of the study of/education in religions. More recently, they co-authored articles on the relationship between Religious Studies and Religious Education and the role of feminist praxis in both. Her publications include *Tradition and Liberation: The Hindu Tradition in the Indian Women's Movement* (Curzon, 1999), *Interpretations of the Bhagavad-Gita and Images of the Hindu Tradition: The Song of the Lord* (Routledge, 2006) and co-editorship of *The Routledge Encyclopedia of Hinduism* (Routledge, 2008) along with, for example, articles on the legacy of Edwin Arnold and religion in the Indian Army (*Religions of South Asia*, 2009, 2014, 2015).

Sean Whittle

is a Visiting Research Fellow at St Mary's University in Twickenham. He is also a Research Associate with the CRDCE, with Professor Gerald Grace. He also held a Fellowship at Heythrop College, University of London. Alongside these academic roles he works part-time as a secondary school RE teacher at Gumley House FCJ Catholic School in West London. He completed his doctoral studies at the Institute of Education – UCL, defending a thesis on the theory or philosophy of Catholic education. His book, *A Theory of Catholic Education* (Bloomsbury, 2014), presents a robust philosophy of Catholic education that draws heavily on insights from Karl Rahner. Dr. Whittle controversially argues in support of a non-confessional theory of Catholic education. In December 2016 Routledge published *Vatican II and New Thinking about Catholic Education*, which is a collection of essays edited by Dr. Whittle on the impact and legacy of *Gravissimum Educationis*. In 2018 he published two edited volumes *Researching Catholic Education* (Springer) and *Religious Education in Catholic schools in the UK and Ireland* (Peter Lang). He completed a Post-doctoral Research Fellowship at Brunel University on the Religious Literacy Project with Dr. David Aldridge, Professor Gert Biesta and Dr. Pat Hannam. In recent years he has been collaborating with other academics working in the field of Catholic education in order to create the Network for Researchers in Catholic Education.

The Forgotten Dimensions of Religious Education

Gert Biesta and Patricia Hannam

Abstract

In this introductory chapter we provide a rationale for the book, focusing on the reason why 'religion' and 'education' may well be seen as forgotten dimensions in contemporary discussions about religious education. We also provide a brief summary of each chapter to show the main topics and lines of thought of the book.

Keywords

religion – education – religious education – educational aims – educational purposes

In this book we bring together ten essays that engage with questions concerning religious education. We have, provocatively but with a question mark, suggested that 'religion' and 'education' could well be the 'forgotten dimensions' of religious education. The reason for making this suggestion, has to do with the fact that, despite ongoing scholarly, policy and practical interest in religious education in the UK and elsewhere, it is remarkable that many contributions seek to find their point of orientation *outside* of the domain of religious education itself.

In recent years there has been significant work in religious education that takes inspiration from, for example, anthropology (see, for example, Jackson, 1997, 2000, 2004a, 2004b, 2006, 2012), the theory of knowledge (see, for example, Wright, 1997, 1998, 1999, 2000, 2003, 2007), and sociology (see, for example, Clarke & Woodhead, 2015; Dinham, & Francis, 2015; Dinham & Shaw, 2015). This work has made important contributions to the theory and practice of religious education, but there are two potential downsides.

One is that anthropological, epistemological and sociological accounts of religion tend to approach religion as a social, cultural or philosophical phenomenon that is to be studied from the 'outside,' so to speak. While it is of course entirely legitimate to do so, such an approach is significantly different from engaging with religion from the 'inside,' that is, as a lived, meaningful reality. The second downside is that such work often leads to agendas and desiderata for education – it articulates, for example, what religious education should aim to achieve or what should be on the curriculum of religious education – without engaging sufficiently with the integrity of education itself. It tries to articulate what education is *for*, whilst forgetting to engage with the question what education *is*. In precisely this sense, then, there is a risk that 'religion' and 'education' become overlooked and end up as the 'missing dimensions' in the conversation about religious education.

The essays brought together in this book are based on presentations given at a seminar we organised in 2017 in which we invited the participants to engage with these 'missing dimensions' of religious education. In some cases, we asked presenters to focus on the educational dimensions of religious education and on the 'integrity' of education itself. This included questions such as: What is this 'thing' called education? What is it for? What does it seek to make possible? What is it not? In other cases, we asked presenters to focus on the religious dimensions of religious education, including matters of theology. This included questions such as: What 'is' religion? What is it not? Is it a singular or a plural category? What does religion look like from the 'inside'? Given that all presenters have an active interest in religious education, including active involvement in religious education and teacher education for religious education, it is not surprising that they also engaged with religious education itself and with the implications for religious education of taking 'education' and 'religion' more seriously.

Of course, the contributions in this book don't have the ambition to speak the final word about matters of religion and education in religious education. But we do hope that our collective effort helps to open up and inform a slightly different conversation about the theory and practice of religious education – one that sees education as more than just a vehicle for conveying curricular content or achieving educational aims, and that sees religion as more than an object of study but as this living reality that can be meaningfully inhabited and actually *is* meaningfully inhabited by many people around the world in a variety of different ways.

This means that in general the chapters are of a reflective nature. They do not report on empirical research, but try to respond meaningfully to the more fundamental questions about the role, status and position of religion and education in religious education. Such discussions can not take place in a vacuum, so the chapters all bear traces from the authors' experience with the dynamics and practicalities of religious education as well. Given that all contributors work in the UK, it is therefore not surprising that this forms a background against which authors have engaged with the more fundamental questions in the field. The book is, however, not a discussion of recent developments in UK policy and practice, but uses that as a background from which to explore the role and position of religion and education in religious education. We anticipate that readers who are familiar with other (national) contexts and settings will be able to make productive translations to their own situations.

While we could have taken out all the references to the seminar where the conversation about the topics of this book started, we felt that keeping these references in gives a more authentic depiction of the conversations that have informed the chapters in this book. It locates the book, in other words, in space and time, which not only gives the book a particular flavour, so we hope, but also conveys the message that this book is not the final word on 'religion' and 'education,' but rather a concerted attempt at bringing these issues to the table. In other words, the book is meant as a starter for such a conversation, and definitely not an end point. So, what then is there to find in this book?

In Chapter 1, called "Education, Education, Education: Reflections on a Missing Dimension," Gert Biesta suggests that education always needs to orient itself to three 'domains of purpose,' to which he refers as qualification, socialisation and subjectification. In the chapter he explores the implications of such an understanding of education for the field of religious education. He focuses specifically on the distinction between socialisation and subjectification, as both 'modalities' of education have to do with the formation of the student as person. Whereas socialisation is engaged with the formation of the student from the 'outside,' which can be understood as a process of cultivation, subjectification is the process where, as educators, we encourage students to take up their own subject-ness, that is, to become subjects of their own life, rather than objects of what other people or forces may want them to be. He suggests that the distinction between socialisation and subjectification is of particular significance for religious education, as it can help to see that taking religion seriously does not necessarily lead to strong forms of religious socialisation.

In Chapter 2, "Education as a Social Practice," Ruth Heilbronn draws on the work of John Dewey in arguing that to promote socially democratic values in education is to draw on a view of what a democratic culture should be. With Dewey she suggests that individuals are embedded in the social and that the social is made of, by and with them. In studying different religions and religious practices students thus become open to the possibility of different ways of conceiving the world. An inclusive and democratic society, so she argues, requires citizens who are at home in a culture that values diversity. A capacity for ethical deliberation is important for this and can be fostered through dialogical pedagogy. She concludes that at its best religious education can create a space for the development and maintenance of critical faculties and sympathetic imagination.

In Chapter 3, "Education as Belonging to a Subject Matter," David Aldridge sets out a pedagogy of 'belonging' for religious education. Aldridge draws on the perspective of philosophical hermeneutics to elaborate the intentional relation of teacher, student and subject matter in the event of understanding. He proposes that dialogue as an existential form has an educational significance that is further complicated when transferred into the 'ontic' situation in which the roles of teacher and student are formally assumed. He also considers the possibility of belonging as what he refers to as an educational 'ethic.' He concludes by arguing that the model of belonging applies as much to the encounter with the 'curriculum' as to the classroom situation, and draws out some implications for the 'questionability' of religious education.

In Chapter 4, "Religion, Reductionism and Pedagogical Reduction," David Lewin addresses questions around educational representation. Starting from the ambition to encourage others to develop a rich understanding of religion(s), he asks what is involved in the selections and simplifications of religious traditions for educational purposes, and also how these generalisations and constructions can be justified. Lewin addresses these questions by developing and applying a theory of *pedagogical reduction*. In doing so, he contrasts the educationally constructive notion of pedagogical reduction to what is often taken to be problematic in understanding religion, namely *reductionism*. He proposes that understanding religion entails the complex pedagogical practices of the give and take of pedagogical reduction.

In Chapter 5, "'Buddhism Is Not a Religion, but Paganism Is': The Applicability of the Concept of 'Religion' to Dharmic and Nature-Based Traditions, and the Implications for Religious Education," Denise Cush and Catherine Robinson explore the concept of religion in popular, academic and adherent usage, and in particular whether it is at all helpful when applied to Dharmic or Nature-based traditions. Problems include the homogenisation of diversity and the construction of separate and unified systems of beliefs and practices which have affected portrayals of 'Eastern' traditions, including in religious education. They conclude by examining the importance for religious education of opening up the debate about what is meant by 'religion,' and of including the study of Dharmic traditions, a wider range of worldviews and new forms of 'being religious' from an early age.

Chapter 6, "Teaching about Islam: From Essentialism to Hermeneutics," contains an interview Gert Biesta conducted with Farid Panjwani and Lynn Revell, in which they explore the complexities of teaching about Islam, particularly in light of the risk of relying on essentialist notions of what 'Islam' is supposed to be. Together they explore different manifestations of such essentialism and discuss the potential of a hermeneutic approach.

In Chapter 7, "On the Precarious Role of Theology in Religious Education," Sean Whittle focuses on religious education in Catholic schools to argue that, despite first impressions, theology plays a precarious role. He presents an analysis of what theology typically involves and then argues that this reveals how, in religious education, there is a serious under-emphasis on the living faith that underpins the academic theology that is part-and-parcel of these lessons. Through drawing on insights from Biesta and Hannam he proposes that the role of theology in religious education is to raise the consciousness or awareness of children and young people. This will help them to know and understand how living the religious life well is a desirable way of being a grown up in the world.

In Chapter 8, "Implicit Knowledge Structures in English Religious Studies Public Exam Questions: How Exam Questions Frame Knowledge, the Experience of Learning, and Pedagogy," Bob Bowie provides an analysis of religious education through a study of the principle question structure used in exams, and the kind of answer responses that can become norms. He examines implicit knowledge structures that prefer binary argumentation rather than nuanced and contextual discussion, literalism and proof-texting with sacred texts rather than polyphonic multidimensionality and contextual readings, and contradictory rather than compatible differences. Through this he shows that the question structures in exams assert a kind of knowledge in religious education constructed by and for examinations rather than related to disciplinary knowledge and forms of religious knowing.

In Chapter 9, "What Should Religious Education Seek to Achieve in the Public Sphere?," Patricia Hannam presents a case for religious education taking an interested position in relation to action in plurality. Outlining how the public sphere, as well as how religion itself, are conceptualised , her argument develops through emphasising that religious education should make an educational contribution to education in the public sphere which, among other things, raises the question of education's relationship with the public sphere. Against this background, she shows some new possibilities for religious education, where education is seen in relation to bringing the child to action in plurality, rather than only to reason. In outlining these new possibilities, she aims to make visible the significance of including the existential response to what it means to live a religious life for the public sphere.

In Chapter 10, Joyce Miller provides reflections on the seminar on *"Religion and Education: The Forgotten Dimensions of Religious Education,"* and, in doing so, opens up a conversation with the authors in this book. Miller provides a reflection on the key conference themes of education, religion and religious education. She argues that religious education is heading towards crisis and that radical changes must be made. A renewed vision for the subject is required that will encompass religion and worldviews and provide a holistic, objective and inclusive approach for all young people. Biesta's concept of 'subjectification' is endorsed and it is argued that a new pedagogy of relationality – with the 'other,' the 'other-than human' and the 'more-than-human' – can provide the theoretical basis for the exploration of religion, secularity, spirituality and worldviews.

We conclude the book with a brief afterword in which we summarise some of the key insights from the different contributions and outline issues for further investigation.

References

Clarke, C., & Woodhead, L. (2015). *A new settlement: Religion and belief in schools.* Westminster Faith Debates.

Dinham, A., & Francis, M. (Eds.). (2015). *Religious literacy in policy and practice.* Policy Press.

Dinham, A., & Shaw, M. (2015). *RE for real: The future of teaching and learning about religion and belief.* Goldsmiths.

Jackson, R. (1997). *Religious education: An interpretive approach.* Hodder & Stoughton.

Jackson, R. (2000). The Warwick religious education project: The interpretive approach to religious education. In M. Grimmitt (Ed.), *Pedagogies of religious education: Case studies in the research and development of good pedagogic practice in RE* (pp. 130–152). McCrimmons.

Jackson, R. (2004a). *Rethinking religious education and plurality: Issues in religious diversity and pedagogy.* Routledge Falmer.

Jackson, R. (2004b). Studying religious diversity in public education: An interpretive approach to religious and intercultural understanding. *Religion & Education, 31*(2), 1–20.

Jackson, R. (2005). Intercultural education, religious plurality and teaching for tolerance: Interpretive and dialogical approaches. *Intercultural Education and Religious Plurality: Oslo Occasional Papers, 1,* 5–13.

Jackson, R. (2006). Understanding religious diversity in a plural world: The interpretive approach. In M. de Souza, G. Durka, K. Engebretson, R. Jackson, & A. McGrady (Eds.), *International handbook of the religious, moral and spiritual dimensions in education* (pp. 399–414). Springer.

Jackson, R. (2012). The interpretive approach to religious education: Challenging Thompson's interpretation. *Journal of Beliefs and Values, 33*(1), 1–9.

Wright, A. (1997). The hermeneutics of modern religious education. *Journal of Beliefs and Values, 18*(2), 203–216.

Wright, A. (1998). Hermeneutics and religious understanding: Towards a critical theory for religious education. *Journal of Beliefs and Values, 19*(1), 59–70.

Wright, A. (1999). *Discerning the spirit.* Culham College Institute.

Wright, A. (2000). The spiritual education project: Cultivating spiritual and religious literacy through a critical pedagogy of religious education. In M. Grimmitt (Ed.), *Pedagogies of religious education: Case studies in the research and development of good pedagogic practice in RE* (pp. 179–187). McCrimmons.

Wright, A. (2003). The contours of critical religious education: Knowledge, wisdom, truth. *British Journal of Religious Education, 25*(4), 279–291.

Wright, A. (2007). *Critical religious education, multiculturalism and the pursuit of truth.* University of Wales Press.

CHAPTER 1

Education, Education, Education: Reflections on a Missing Dimension

Gert Biesta

Abstract

In this chapter I suggest that education always needs to orient itself in relation to three purposes or domains of purpose. I refer to these as qualification, socialisation and subjectification and discuss what the three might mean in the domain of religious education. I focus specifically on the distinction between socialisation and subjectification, as both 'modalities' of education have to do with the formation of the student as person. Whereas socialisation is engaged with the formation of the student from the 'outside,' which can be understood as a process of cultivation, subjectification is the process where, as educators, we encourage students to take up their own subject-ness, that is, to become subjects of their own life, rather than objects of what other people or forces may want them to be. That our existence as subject is called into being from the outside, suggests the importance of education vis-à-vis the question of our existence as subject and shows that religion and education may be more closely connected than what is often assumed.

Keywords

purposes of education – learnification – religious education – cultivation – subjectification

1   Introduction

The presentation upon which this chapter is based, was given a few days after a gunman killed 58 people and wounded 413 in Las Vegas, USA, on 1 October

2017, killing himself afterwards. The FBI investigation found "no single or clear motivating factor" for the killings, and closed the case early in 2019 with the motive remaining officially 'undetermined.' Events like these not just raise questions about motive. They also raise educational questions, not least the question how someone's life can unfold in such a way that it ends like this. Or as the headline of one UK newspaper put it: "What turned Mr Normal into a mass killer?" (Daily Mail, 3 October 2017).

It would be one thing to understand why 'Mr Normal' turned into a mass killer. It would still be another question to figure out what education might do – or in this case: could have done – to prevent this from happening. This is a legitimate question and one that educators should be concerned about. Yet, we also know that it is an impossible ambition to think that we, as educators, *can* totally control who our students will become and also that we *should try* to control this. After all, total control turns students into objects and leaves no place for their own capacity to act, that is, for their own freedom. Education has something to do with this dilemma or, as it is known in the educational literature, with this paradox: that while, as educators we do want to *influence* our students, we do not want to fully *determine* their thoughts, feelings and actions. It is the question of "Führen oder Wachsenlassen," as Theodor Litt (1927) put it – to direct or to let grow.

In this chapter I want to offer a few reflections on education that may be helpful in considering what the field of religious education is, what it can be and what it might be. The reason why I think that education may be a 'missing dimension' of religious education, is because in the English speaking world the question of education is often either seen as a merely practical question – the question of 'how' to teaching religion, for example – or is tackled in terms of the rather ubiquitous but in my view extremely unhelpful language of 'teaching and learning.' I wish to suggest that the educational dimension of religious education is not just about practical matters but raises important intellectual and existential issues that are worthy of further consideration.

What is rather unfortunate is that the English language only seems to have one word – education – whereas in Continental languages such as German, there are a number of different words to speak about and 'in' education. This lies behind my title, as I will suggest in what is to follow that the word 'education' can actually be translated into three different German words and that getting a sense of the distinctions that these words denote can be very helpful for a more precise understanding of what the educational dimensions of religious education might be. However, I would like to start my reflections with another ubiquitous word in the vocabulary of English-speaking education, namely the word 'learning.'

2   The Language of Learning and the 'Learnification' of Education

The word 'learning' has become a very central word in contemporary discussions about education. One could even argue that the rise of the language of learning stands for a paradigm shift in education. Many have actually welcomed this shift, particularly because of the ambition to counter a one-sided emphasis on teaching and, more specifically, on the input side of education, without paying sufficient attention to what all this does on the side of pupils and students (see, for example, Barr & Tagg, 1995).

As a result, pupils and students are now often being referred to as 'learners,' schools as 'places for learning,' and classrooms as 'learning communities,' while teaching has been recategorized as the act of 'facilitating learning.' The language of learning is also very visible in the rebranding of adult education as 'lifelong learning.' I have suggested to refer to the remarkable rise of the language of learning as the 'learnification' of educational discourse and practice (see, for example, Biesta, 2010), and I have deliberately chosen a rather awkward and in a sense even ugly term because I think that the learnification of education is quite problematic from an educational point of view.

While everyone is, of course, free to learn, and while we can safely say that learning can happen anytime and anywhere, the education question is a much more precise question than what can be captured with the language of learning. A blunt but nonetheless accurate way to state the problem is that the point of education can never be that pupils or students just learn. The point of education rather is that pupils and students learn something, learn it for a reason and learn it from someone, that is, in and through educational relationships. These three issues – content, purpose, and relationships – distinguish the language of education from the language of learning.

This is not to suggest, of course, that when teachers, policy makers, researchers or students themselves speak the language of learning, content and relationships are absent and the whole endeavour is directionless. It rather is that under the language of learning it is far more difficult to keep questions of content, purpose and relationships into view. As a result, it becomes easier for other forces to take over, such as the now prominent but rather meaningless idea that education should be about the effective production of measurable learning outcomes in order to drive up test scores and, through this, a country's position in the PISA rankings.

3   Starting with the Question of Purpose

Of the three questions that distinguish an educational discourse from a learning discourse, the question of purpose is the first question, because it is only when we have an answer to the question what we think that our educational endeavours are *for* that we can begin to say something about the content that students should encounter and engage with in order to make this possible and about the most meaningful ways in which educational relationships can be put to work.

What is important to see, however, is that unlike many other fields of human practice, education's purpose is not singular. Rather it can be argued that education should always be concerned about and hence orientated towards three different purposes or 'domains of purpose' (for this phrase see, e.g., Biesta, 2010), to which I have referred as (1) qualification, (2) socialisation and (3) subjectification. Whereas the German language has three different and rather precise words to denote these different domains of educational purpose – namely 'Ausbildung,' 'Bildung' and 'Erziehung' – in English they all end up as the single word 'education.'[1] In English, then, we are stuck with the suggestion that the purpose of education is education, education and education![2]

At one level the distinction between three domains of educational purpose is not really difficult to understand, although there are some further nuances that make the discussion rather more complicated (see also Biesta, 2020, in press), but also more relevant for religious education, as I will argue below. The domain of qualification has to do with the presentation and acquisition of knowledge and skills. This is not just in order to obtain qualifications (in the plural) but first and foremost because knowledge and skills are important for the agency of individuals, that is, for their capacity to act and, more specifically, to act in knowledgeable and skilful ways.

Education's task is, however, not confined to knowledge and skills but also plays an important role in socialisation, that is, in providing pupils and students with orientation, that is, with an introduction into traditions, cultures and practices so that they know 'their way around,' so to speak. Both qualification and socialisation are important in education for working life; but they are also important to provide children and young people with the knowledge, skills and orientation to live their lives in complex, modern societies. The third domain, that of subjectification, concerns the ways in which education contributes to the formation of the student as person – not as an object we try to influence from the 'outside,' so to speak, but as subject in their own right.

4   A Threefold Educational Prism

Acknowledging that education has legitimate work to do in each of these domains, already helps in having a much more informed and refined discussion about education – something that is virtually impossible if we only insist that education should make pupils and students learn. The three domains of purpose stand for a broad conception of educational quality in which it is acknowledged that good education needs to be concerned about qualification, socialisation and subjectification.

Such a broad view of what matters in education also helps to reveal what is wrong with one-sided conceptions of education. I am inclined to think that we suffer most from a one-sided emphasis on qualification, to the detriment of the important work that education has to do vis-à-vis socialisation and subjectification. But education which only focuses on socialisation – particularly 'strong' socialisation into particular socio-cultural 'orders' – is also one-sided, as is education that only has a concern for the subject-ness of students but doesn't care about their knowledge, skills and sense of orientation.

Looking at education through this threefold 'prism' also helps to see why three-dimensional thinking and doing is of the utmost importance in research, policy and practice. It provides the basis for a meaningful critique of the obsession with effectiveness, not just because it can ask the almost entirely absent question what education should be effective *for* – after all, effectiveness in the domain of qualification is likely to be something very different from effectiveness in the domain of socialisation or the domain of subjectification. The threefold 'prism' also quickly reveals that effectiveness always has a price, particularly that a push on what may work for one domain may actually not work for another domain or may actually work to the detriment of other domains.

This doesn't make things easier, but it does make research and policy more relevant for education, and more 'adjusted' to the unique complexity of education. The threefold 'prism' also helps to get a much better appreciation of the complex work of teachers if, that is, in all their actions they seek to find a meaningful balance between what can and should be achieved in each of the three domains. It immediately shows that this is not a matter of just following 'evidence,' because such evidence is in most cases constructed one-dimensionally; teaching always requires situated judgement about what is to be done here and now bearing in mind the threefold purpose of education.

5   A Threefold Approach to Religious Education

The threefold 'prism' is also helpful in considering questions about religious education. While it may not immediately resolve the more difficult questions about what religious education should be for and what it should be about, it does at least provide a more precise language for considering different options, concerns and considerations. In the domain of qualification religious education has an important role to play in providing pupils and students with knowledge and understanding about religion, religions and the religious, and with the skills to use such knowledge and understanding wisely. This is important work because it helps children and young people to act in knowledgeable ways vis-à-vis religion, religions and the religious (and even grasping the distinction between these notions could itself already be an important part of the qualification task of religious education).

Where it concerns socialisation, there are two different discussions that are relevant here. Socialisation can be understood in a rather 'strong' sense, where the point of socialisation is not that of providing children and young people with orientation into existing religious cultures, traditions and practices, but where the ambition is for them to 'sign up' to particular cultures, traditions, practices or religions. While such a confessional approach to religious education is one manifestation of religious socialisation – and in my view a problematic one because it basically treats students only as objects to be recruited, not as subjects in their own right – the more meaningful 'modality' of religious socialisation is that of providing orientation, which we might characterise as a 'weak' form of socialisation.

Here I think that religious education has important (and complex) work to do as well, not just in providing pupils and students with knowledge about religion, religions and the religious, but with a sense of 'knowing one's way around,' so to speak. If qualification looks at religion(s) from the outside, socialisation seeks to bring a perspective from the inside – at least in encountering what it might mean, how it might feel, what there is to experience, from the 'inside' of religious traditions and practices. Whether one wishes this to be part of religious education is, of course, a matter for further discussion. But that this is a legitimate and 'possible' educational ambition is what the threefold prism helps to bring into view.

This also means, however, that religious education can never stop there; religious education can never just consider pupils and students as 'objects' of educational interventions (to use a rather crude formulation). Religious education, if it takes its educational dimension seriously, always needs to consider the subject-ness of pupils and students. In order to figure out what that might mean, I wish to say a few more things about the difference between socialisation and subjectification and the different 'modalities' of educational action that are related to this.

6   Socialisation and Subjectification: A Modern Distinction

What is at stake in the idea of subjectification and in education's interest in and concern for subjectification, is the question of human freedom. This is about our freedom to act or to refrain from action, to say yes or no to what we encounter, to stay or walk away from the situations we find ourselves in, to go with the flow or offer resistance. Put in these terms it is clear that freedom is not a theoretical construct or a philosophical ideal, but a thoroughly existential matter – a possibility we encounter at some point in our own life, and something we also encounter in meeting and interacting with other human beings.

For a long time in the history of the West, education's interest in freedom was, as Werner Jaeger (1965) has put it, 'aristocratic' rather than 'democratic.' Education was there to provide those who were *already* free – wealthy men, in most cases – with the cultural and intellectual resources to work on their own perfection. For the rest of the population – women, labourers and slaves – freedom was seen as a problem that needed to be overcome or 'contained' through (strong) training, (strong) socialisation and (strong) moralisation, sometimes with 'carrots' but more often with 'sticks.'

A crucial change took place with the Enlightenment where education's interest shifted from the 'perfection' of those who were *already* free to the 'emancipation' of those who were not yet free. Kant's famous formulation of the 'motto' of the Enlightenment as having the courage to make use of one's own understanding suggested a democratic educational orientation towards encouraging *everyone* to make use of their understanding, that is, to think for themselves, draw their own conclusions and act upon them, rather than following other people's orders. It is precisely here that subjectification becomes an educational 'theme' or 'concern' and hence the distinction between education as socialisation and education as subjectification becomes 'possible,' so to speak.

For Kant this did make education into a paradoxical endeavour, which he expressed in the question 'How do I cultivate freedom through coercion?'[3] As long as one thinks of education as cultivation – the cultivation of a human 'organism' towards his or her own freedom – the educational interest in this freedom is indeed paradoxical, as if we can *make* children and young people free, as if, as educators, we can *produce* this freedom. Kant's paradox exists, however, because he tried to think subjectification 'in terms of' socialisation. A helpful way out of this paradox can be found in Dietrich Benner's suggestion to understand the educational work of subjectification not in terms of cultivation but as 'Aufforderung zur Selbsttätigkeit' (see Benner, 2015).

7   Education beyond Cultivation: The Work of *Erziehung*

'Aufforderung' is not the cultivation of an object – which is a problem with Kant's formulation – but can better be understood as a summoning, as encouragement, one might say, that speaks to the child or young person *as* subject.[4] 'Selbsttätigkeit,' which literally means self-action, is not the injunction to be active but to be(come) *self*-active. In more everyday language this is not about becoming *your*self, and particularly not about being yourself in the simplistic sense of just doing what you want to do, but about being *a* self, being a subject of your own life.

'Aufforderung zur Selbsttätigkeit,' summoning the child or young person to be a self (Benner), arousing a desire in children and young people to exist as subject of their own life (Biesta, 2017, chapter 1), refusing children and young people the comfort of *not* being a subject (Rancière, 2010), is what education as subjectification is about. It is, therefore, not about the educational production of the subject – in which the subject would be reduced to an object – but is about bringing the subject-ness of the child or young person 'into play,' so to speak; helping the child or young person not to forget that they *can* exist as subject.[5]

This is not to suggest that cultivation should play no role in education. On the contrary, there is also important work to do by educators in providing the new generation with access to all the cultural resources that humankind has developed over the ages. This is the work of what in German is called 'Bildung,' and comes quite close to what I have discussed as 'socialisation.' It is about initiating children and young people into existing traditions and practices, and encouraging them to find their own place within them. We might say, therefore, that 'Bildung' has important work to do in helping children and young people to find an identity, that is, a sense of an answer to the question who they are – or in the singular: Who am I?

Identity, understood in these terms, is very much about identification: what do I (wish to) identity with, and how might others identify me. The question of subjectification – linked to the educational work of 'Erziehung' – is, however, not about how we may come to an answer to the question who we are. The question of subjectification, and the work of 'Erziehung,' is focused on a different question, namely the question *how* we are, *how* we are going to be. Or in more everyday language: it is the question what I will do with my identity and, also, what I will do with all the knowledge and skills I have acquired.

8   Who Is the 'I'? Considering Two Subject Positions

While we may raise this question ourselves – for example by asking: What will I do with my talents?, What will I do with everything I have acquired?, What will I do with how I have become cultivated?, and even: What will I do with my life? – more often than not this question becomes relevant, or even acute, when we encounter a question, an appeal or even a demand that comes to us from the 'outside' of from 'elsewhere.' This seems to suggest, then, that with regard to the question of the (existence of the) 'I' there are two different 'subject positions' to consider. Put briefly, it is about the distinction between an 'I' who raises questions and an 'I' who is 'in question.'

The first option is one that we are probably quite familiar with. One could even argue that this option is the one that informs much of contemporary education. The 'I' here is the one who asks questions and who tries to make sense of the (social and natural) world 'outside' of itself. We could call this 'I' a learner, that is, someone who is trying to learn about the world. This is of course part of how we exist as human beings. As learners, as the ones who ask questions and seek answers, we are, in a sense, before the world – temporally and spatially – which means that the world, in this set up, appears as an object of my attempts at understanding and comprehension.

Leading questions here are 'How can I understand all this?,' 'How can I make sense of all this?' These are important questions, for life and for education. Yet the idea which I have been pursuing in this chapter can be summarised by saying that this is not the only way in which we can conceive of ourselves 'in the world'; it is not the only way in which we can think about our existence. In addition to, or next to, us being an 'I' who asks questions and seeks answers, there is another 'I' or another subject position, that doesn't originate from me, but where the 'I' is the one who is addressed, who is put in question.

Zygmunt Bauman in his book *Postmodern Ethics* (Bauman, 1993) summarises this insight very well with his suggestion that 'responsibility is the first reality of the self.' Bauman's point here is not that we are ethical beings who ought to be responsible. He rather seeks to highlight that it is actually only in situations where we encounter 'a' responsibility that our 'I' begins to matter, or more specifically: that my 'I' begins to matter. In such situations, as Emmanuel Levinas has put it, we are, in a sense, 'awakened' by the other, and it is only in such events that our 'Ego' (Levinas), our 'I' begins to gain significance.

Here the leading question is not that of understanding or meaning – How can I understand? How can I make sense? – but the question rather is: What is this asking from me?, What is this trying to say to me?, and perhaps even: What is this trying to teach me? This is not, then, the moment where the individual asserts itself into the world as meaning-maker or learner. it rather is the moment where the 'I' as subject is called into the world, called into existence in the world.

This, then, is not a matter of cultivation of an object (Bildung), but of calling a subject into its subject-ness (Erziehung), a subject-ness that doesn't take place with oneself but takes place 'outside' of oneself, in and with the world.

It is important to see that while educators may be the ones who are involved in this calling or even issue the call, they are definitely not the only or single 'callers.' What makes more sense is to think of the work of educators as that of trying to alert students to the world that may be calling them. Here we can find support in the etymology of the word education which can be read as ex-ducere, that is, as leading out or leading away from oneself, towards the world.[6]

Klaus Prange (2015) has actually suggested that 'pointing,' and more specifically pointing towards the world, is the most basic gesture or operation (his term) of all education, something which can also be found in the Dutch word for teaching, which is onderwijzen where 'wijzen' means pointing. Patricia Hannam (2018), taking inspiration from Simone Weil, has suggested that the first educational 'act' is that of bringing the child to attention which, in the context of what I have been suggesting in this chapter, is first and foremost about bring the world to the attention of the child. What the world will be asking from the child is, of course, not for the teacher to determine, but for the child to find out.

9   Concluding Comments

In this chapter I have tried to offer some reflections on the educational dimension of religious education. I have tried to show that there is more to education than learning or 'teaching-and-learning' and that one way to move 'beyond learning' (Biesta, 2006) is to acknowledge that there are three legitimate domains for education to be concerned with: the domain of qualification, the domain of socialisation and the domain of subjectification. Religious education can, of course, just try to confine itself to the domain of qualification. In that case religion only appears as an object of knowledge and the student remains, in a sense, 'outside' of this object of study.

When religious education tries to confine itself to socialisation, religion appears as practice or tradition, but not just as practice or tradition to be studied from the 'outside,' but also as practice and tradition to be encountered and experienced from the 'inside,' so to speak. While this may allow for more meaningful encounters with religion, the risk here is that religious education becomes a form of strong socialisation, where the sole ambition becomes that of making sure that children and young people 'sign up' to a particular religious tradition. From an educational perspective, or at least the one I have presented in this chapter, the problem here is that the child or young person would ultimately disappear from the scene – would become an object of socialisation, not a subject of education.

This is where a third option for religious education comes into view, that of religious education that takes up the challenge of subjectification, that is, of taking the subject-ness of the student seriously. This, as I have tried to make clear, is not a matter of identity, of finding one's self, so to speak, but a matter of existence, of existing in and with the world, 'outside' of oneself. This is not a matter of learning and also not a matter of cultivation, but is thoroughly existential – it is about how we try to exist in and with the world and, more specifically, how the world, social and natural, calls us (in)to existence. I have suggested that this is at the heart of what education is about and should be about. At the same time, it will not be too difficult to recognise a theological theme in this line of thinking.[7] This leads me to conclude, then, that a proper engagement with the 'E' in 'RE' may actually reveal a much more intimate connection with the 'R' in RE than what a relegation of the 'E' to merely practical matters may make visible.

Notes

1   I invite the reader to put the three words in Google translate. The last time I tried this, the first English translation that was suggested for each of them was, indeed, 'education' (accessed 10 February 2020).
2   Readers who still remember Tony Blair may also remember that the 'three priorities' he defined for his government were indeed 'education, education, education,' although I doubt that he had the German equivalents in mind when he announced this.
3   In German it reads: 'Wie kultiviere ich die Freiheit bei dem Zwange?' (Kant, 1982, p. 711).
4   Such speaking can be counterfactual – it can go against all the evidence we have in front of us – think for example of when parents speak to their new-born baby, where there is as yet little evidence that this baby is a subject, let alone that it is a subject who is capable of understanding the meaning of what his or her parents are saying. Yet it is the very approaching of the baby as if it were a subject that opens up the possibility for its future existence as subject. On the dynamics of this 'gesture' see Biesta (2017, chapter 5).
5   This shows that the educational gesture here is fundamentally non-affirmative – another helpful phrase from Benner (1995) – because the educator is not telling the child or young person how they should become, what they should do with their freedom, which 'template' or 'image' they should adopt and aspire to, which all would be instances of affirmative education.
6   The German word 'Erziehen' has a similar etymology, where 'ziehen' literally means to 'pull.' The root of the word 'Bildung,' on the other hand, is the word 'Bild,' which means image and is therefore closer to holding up an image towards which children and young people should be cultivated or towards which they should cultivate themselves.
7   Sean Whittle's chapter in this collection explores this connection in more detail.

References

Barr, R. B., & Tagg, J. (1995). From teaching to learning: A new paradigm for undergraduate education. *Change*, November/December, 13–25.

Bauman, Z. (1993). *Postmodern ethics.* Basil Blackwell.

Benner, D. (1995). Bildsamkeit und Bestimmung. Zu Fragestellung und Ansatz nichtaffirmativer Bildungstheorie. In *Studien zur Theorie der Erziehung und Bildung, Bd. 2* (pp. 141–159). Weinheim: Juventa.

Benner, D. (2015). *Allgemeine Pädagogik* (8th ed.). Juventa.

Biesta, G. (2006). *Beyond learning: Democratic education for a human future.* Routledge.

Biesta, G. (2010). *Good education in an age of measurement: Ethics, politics, democracy.* Routledge.

Biesta, G. (2017). *The rediscovery of teaching.* Routledge.

Biesta, G. (2020). Risking ourselves in education: Qualification, socialisation and subjectification revisited. *Educational Theory, 70*(1), 89–104.

Biesta, G. (in press). Can the prevailing description of educational reality be considered complete? On the Parks-Eichmann paradox, spooky action at a distance, and a missing dimension in the theory of education. *Policy Futures in Education.*

Hannam, P. (2018). *Religious education and the public sphere.* Routledge.

Jaeger, W. (1965). *Paideia: Archaic Greece. The mind of Athens.* Oxford University Press.

Kant, I. (1982). Über Pädagogik. In I. Kant (Ed.), *Schriften zur Anthropologie, Geschichtsphilosophie, Politik und Pädagogik* (pp. 695–761). Insel Verlag.

Litt, Th. (1929). *Führen oder Wachsenlassen. Eine Erörterung des pädagogischen Grundproblems.* T.G.Teubner.

Prange, K. (2005). *Die Zeigestruktur der Erziehung: Grundriss der operativen Pädagogik.* Ferdinand Schöningh.

Rancière, J. (2010). On ignorant schoolmasters. In C. Bingham & G. J. J. Biesta (Eds.), *Jacques Rancière: Education, truth, emancipation* (pp. 1–24). Continuum.

CHAPTER 2

Education as Social Practice

Ruth Heilbronn

Abstract

This chapter draws particularly on the work of John Dewey in arguing that to promote socially democratic values is to draw on a view of what a democratic culture should be. Individuals are embedded in the social and the social is made of, by and with them. In studying different religions and religious practices students become open to the possibility of different ways of conceiving the world. An inclusive and democratic society requires citizens who are at home in a culture that values diversity. A capacity for ethical deliberation is important and can be fostered through dialogical pedagogy. At its best religious education can create a space for the development and maintenance of critical faculties and sympathetic imagination.

Keywords

Dewey – cultures – dialogical pedagogy – diversity – democratic citizenship – sympathetic imagination

1   Introduction

Education is a social practice and as such it is pertinent to ask what role religious education might play in furthering societal aims. This turns on what these aims are, how they are defined, and within what paradigm they sit. Education policies and practices depend on these aims which embody the values which underly curricula choice. It seems evident that schools have an important role to play in imparting values. An inclusive and democratic society requires citizens who are at home in a culture that values diversity. For this to happen, there needs to be familiarity with diverse cultures, and one way into this education is through knowledge of different religious traditions and practices.

In addition to requisite knowledge of different religions and cultures, the ability to participate responsibly and inclusively in civic society requires certain capacities that cannot be developed technically as 'skills' – to listen to others for example requires more than 'listening skills,' since it requires a relational capacity to be open to others. The humanities, including religious education, can play an important role in supporting the development of other necessary capacities, such as the ability to weigh up evidence, to argue rationally to well-founded conclusions. Participation in the social, on micro and macro levels, requires more than these capacities as it needs the ability to judge between competing views, in order to discern the values underlying these views. A capacity for ethical deliberation is therefore important and can be fostered through dialogical pedagogy. At its best religious education is a subject which creates a space for the development and maintenance of critical faculties and sympathetic imagination, which it does through study of different religions and religious practices and through promotion of dialogical pedagogy.

The chapter draws particularly on the work of John Dewey in arguing that to promote socially democratic values is to draw on a view of what a democratic culture should be. Individuals are embedded in the social and the social is made of, by and with them. In studying different religions and religious practices students become open to the possibility of different ways of conceiving the world. When they are encouraged to discuss ethical issues students also gain an understanding of their complexity. When well managed discussions take place on controversial issues in the religious education classroom students have an opportunity to engage in the kind of discussion that respects competing views, and this supports the development of the dispositions needed for social cohesion.

2 Dewey's View of Learning through Experience

Social cohesion starts in school, in the habits that are developed when students experience an education in inclusion and openness to others in their school life. Dewey defined democracy as "more than a form of government; it is primarily a mode of associated living, of conjoint communicated experience" (Dewey, 1916, p. 9). For Dewey, education needs to start in understanding mutual dependency of society and children, in the sense that the young experience and experiment within the social milieu and are also receiving the culture and mediated experience of adults. Key qualities that enable children's development are their flexibility and plasticity. With their social responsiveness, children learn from experience and develop dispositions and habits. Active adjustments to the environment develop into "habits of active use of our surroundings" (Dewey, 1916, p. 52). There can be good or bad habits and both informal and formal education should enable students to develop good habits. From an anthropological standpoint the culture in which a child grows is the sustaining environment that develops habits and dispositions. From the experiential, "settled habits and dispositions develop" (Dewey, 1938, p. 12). What children experience needs to be thought of as their being in a kind of bio-feedback interactivity, which Dewey names 'continuity of experience,' that is "fundamental in the constitution of experience" (Dewey, 1939, p. 31). Continuity of experience is exemplified by growth or growing "not only physically but intellectually and morally" (Dewey, 1939, p. 19).

Without continuity of experience there would be no growth. Dewey's concept of growth is therefore "deeply embedded in his theory of educative experience" (Keall, 2010), which is rooted in moral development. "Education means the enterprise of supplying the conditions which insure growth, or adequacy of life, irrespective of age" (Dewey, 1916, p. 56). These conditions are culturally determined. 'Growth' for Dewey is a normative concept. "Growth itself is the moral end" (Dewey, 1939, p. 181) and to "protect, sustain and direct growth is the chief ideal of education" (Dewey, 1939, p. 402). For Dewey the child acquires a moral sense through learning in all subjects in which she is experimenting or actively engaged with ideas. Growing as 'a moral end' means growing in moral understanding in a specific place and time, with specific people, engaging in specific practices, which is the force of 'culture in the way Dewey meant it to be substituted for experience. This is the contingent culture out of which the child develops habits. This means that everything in school is permeated with ethical import. The school is a place where children learn 'in associated living' to participate democratically in social life. Dewey goes so far as to state that this is the purpose of school in his assertion that "apart from participation in social life, the school has no moral end nor aim" (Dewey, 1909, p. 271). Subjects studied, be they geography, history, mathematics, all carry the values of the curriculum as prepared by policy makers, teachers and other developers, because "the moral purpose [is] universal and dominant in all instruction, whatever the topic" (Dewey, 1909, p. 267). In an appendix to *Moral Principles in Education* (1909) Dewey sets out the parameters of how the school embodies 'moral training' which he outlines under headings. among which he states "the unity of social ethics and school ethics," that "school life should train for many social relations," that "there is no harmonious development of powers apart from social situations," and that "school activities should be typical of social life" (Dewey, 1909, p. 332).

Dewey also pointed us in the right direction in stating that "we must take the child as a member of society in the broadest sense, and demand for and from the schools whatever is necessary to enable the child intelligently to recognize all his social relations and take his part in sustaining them" (Dewey,

1909, p. 8). The purpose of education is to allow the individual child to grow in capacities and also to enable that child to engage as a future citizen. For Dewey these two aims are mutually dependent because this idea cannot be applied to all the members of a society "except where intercourse of man with man is mutual, and except where there is adequate provision for the reconstruction of social habits and institutions by means of wide stimulation arising from equitably distributed interests. And this means a democratic society" (Dewey, 1916, p. 107).

3   Aims of Education

A culture which accepts diverse viewpoints and the rights of individuals, and is open to critical scrutiny, can assist in enabling a democratic outlook. Schools, teachers, parents, carers are channels through which the educational culture is carried, although peers and the entire media environment is also significant. In education a primary way in which a culture is transmitted is through the vehicle of a school curriculum. Evidently changing policies around what should be taught in national curricular reflect underlying political values and beliefs. Religious education as a humanities subject, in common with other arts and humanities subjects affords opportunities for the cultivation of democratic dispositions. However, the scope given to educators in creating the school curriculum can vary. In many current jurisdictions there is limited opportunity for modification at a local level, if the policy culture is predominantly based on a performative norm. Performativity as an underlying educational aim tends towards a curriculum based on delivering measurable outcomes, one which is capable of being reported comparatively. This is the case in many education systems worldwide, where the aims of education are predominantly subsumed to economic ends, related to gaining skills, qualifications and employment in a global economy (Ball, 2000; Apple, 2005). In such systems, pupils are routinely audited to ensure they achieve these skills, as are teachers, to monitor their 'effectiveness' in curricular 'delivery.' There may be a tendency to 'teach to the test' and where the subjects reported on are predominantly Science, Technology and Mathematics (STEM subjects) other areas of the curriculum can be squeezed for time. This is of concern, since at school level at least, the STEM subjects do not readily call on heuristic capacity. RE has to compete against these 'favoured' subjects as do the creative arts.

The emphasis on examination results is an emphasis on each student's individual achievements as tested in examinations and standardised tests. Models of cooperative learning, such as may emerge in group work, are more difficult to test and less routinely examined and reported on. Yet without cooperation the challenges facing young people cannot be met, for example the threat posed by climate change. The young who protest about climate change demonstrate their faith in the solidarity of collective action. From this apparent contradiction, between an education system that in the main rewards individualism and a consciousness that understands cooperation, there emerge different paradigms of what education might be for.

4   Moral Seriousness

Rather than starting from the auditing of achievement in examinations as a fundamental aim of education, we could start by asking questions about the kind of society we hope for and use this as a starting point. In addressing these questions RE has an important role to play. Oakeshott (1972/1989) posed questions about the character of the world which a human new-comer is born into and will inhabit and asked, "What does it mean to become human?" "Which human qualities do we wish to nurture and develop and how could education foster them?" If we start from this viewpoint rather than the economic aim, schools, curricula and the work of teachers would look different from the current model. Richard Pring calls this 'learning to be human' and defines it as involving:

> First the acquisition of knowledge and understanding to help one manage life intelligently; practical capabilities, and a developed sense of community with which our own well-being is connected. [...] Most importantly added to this is the moral dimension in which young persons are enabled to see life as a whole, to think seriously about the life worth living, to recognise excellence and to want to pursue it in the activities they are engaged in. (Pring, 2013, p. 32)

Pring characterises the capacity delineated in this passage as 'moral seriousness' and in his work expresses the view that education should promote and develop it. As well as a "capacity for being serious about life" (Pring, 1997, p. 38), moral seriousness is "a concern to work out what kind of life is worth living" (Pring, 1999, p. 167), and is "caring about values" (Pring, 2013, p. 36). Moral seriousness matters, Pring argues, because it is the essential characteristic of becoming and being a person.[1]

Moral seriousness implies an ethical attitude to others and therefore an awareness of self in relation to others. Schools have a vital role to play in developing the capacity for moral seriousness and it could be argued, with John Dewey, that "only as we interpret school activities with reference to the larger circle of social activities to which they relate do we find any standard for judging their moral significance" (Dewey, 1909, p. 13). With Dewey, it can be claimed that the school is a place with a fundamental moral purpose relating to inducting children into the life of society and preparing them to take their place in the world. To accept the moral purpose of the school and the school as a place where children are together in "a form of associated living," presupposes interacting with people on the basis of mutuality and this means that whether it is explicitly stated or not the school's role is "the development of character through all the agencies, instrumentalities and materials of school life" (Dewey, 1909, p. 3). Dewey believes that the child acquires a moral sense through learning in all subjects in which she is experimenting or actively engaged with ideas, and that "the school is an institution erected by society to contribute to maintaining the life and advancing the welfare of society" (Dewey, 1909, p. 7). The child is "an organic whole, intellectually, socially and morally, as well as physically" (Dewey, 1909, p. 11). This rich view of the child to be educated entails an ethical responsibility on the school to provide an education which will give the child "such possession of himself that he may take charge of himself and in so doing have power to shape and direct social changes" (Dewey, 1909, p. 11). Such an education could be called humanistic, and religious education is one subject component in a humanistic education, which could be contrasted with education in which the emphasis is placed primarily on technical, mathematical and scientific subjects.

Participation in a diverse civic society requires individuals who are educated with certain capacities, one essential being the capacity for moral seriousness. Humanistic education then is not one in which "achievement comes to denote the sort of thing that a well-planned machine can do better than a human being can" (Dewey, 1916, p. 245).

Knowledge is humanistic in quality "because of what it *does* in liberating human intelligence and human sympathy. Any subject matter which accomplishes this result is humane, and any subject matter which does not accomplish it is not even educational" (Dewey, 1916, p. 238). With the idea of education as enabling a sense of moral seriousness towards the world and others another quality is important, that of moral imagination, the ability to step into another person's shoes and see the world through their eyes.

5   Moral Imagination

Humanistic education helps students to develop the capacity for positive social engagement.[2] Martha Nussbaum claims that through the humanities we can develop sympathy and 'moral imagination,' the capacity to more fully put ourselves in another person's situation. When we do this, it is less likely that we will view others as different, or dehumanised and 'othered.' Moral imagination is a source of 'moral seriousness' that enables us to sympathise with others as engaged in our common humanity. Since education is a social undertaking, education for humanistic aims seeks to develop students' capabilities and capacities for social engagement as well as their own individual development.

Having sympathy with another person implies having feelings of pity and sorrow for someone else's misfortune and also having a common feeling with someone in their situation. Lived situations are complex, embodied, situated, contingent. The humanities and the creative subjects are important to the development of an understanding of the complexity of the lived situation. Through sympathetic engagement with characters' situations in a text or a play, or through understanding the different viewpoints on an values issues, such as issues discussed in philosophical enquiries in RE, students can come to exercise moral imagination and develop a sense of moral engagement which is fundamental to the development of democratic citizenship.

Discussion and debate are crucial to developing a critically alert sense, and therefore essential in education. More than this, the kinds of situations and dilemmas that students encounter through the questions raised in religious education lessons when dealing with the areas of values and world religions is often one of moral ambiguity and in considering these situations together students are engaging in "a dramatic rehearsal (in imagination) of various competing lines of action" (Dewey, 1922, p. 132).

> Deliberation is an experiment in finding out what the various lines of possible action are really like ... to see what the resultant action would be like if it were entered upon. But the trial is in imagination, not in overt fact .... An act overtly tried out is irrevocable, its consequences cannot be blotted out. An act tried out in imagination is not final or fatal. It is retrievable. (Dewey, 1922, p. 133)

Engaging in deliberation of this kind, at one remove from people's personal life situations, enables a distance from important issues that need to be aired. Discussions in religious education classes can provide more complex descriptions of moral dilemmas and problems of practical reasoning than examples generated from rules or schema devised for the purpose of testing rules. This can be seen in many schemes of work. An example taken from the Devon Local Authority Agreed Syllabus for KS3 students asks how we make moral choices, under the theme 'Beliefs in Action in the World':

> This enquiry explores how religious and other beliefs affect approaches to moral issues (a) What are moral questions? (b) What are the consequences

of the moral choices we make? (d) What people and organisations help in making moral choices? (c) What are the most important moral values and teachings? (e) How do we decide what is right and wrong? (Devon 2014, p. 13)

Another enquiry in this syllabus asks, 'Where are the answers to life's big questions?' and under the theme 'Authority'

> explores how religions and worldviews express values and commitments in a variety of creative ways (a) How do people express in creative ways their deepest values and commitments? (b) What is meant by truth? (c) Why are, for some people, sacred texts, teachings and places really important? (d) In what ways might religious teachings and beliefs matter today? What can we learn from religions, beliefs and community today? (Devon, 2014, p. 14)

To underscore how well religious education can engage students in reflection on moral issues and prepare them for living in a multi faith and multi-ethnic society the same syllabus treats the theme of Inter-faith Dialogue and

> explores ideas of those aspects of human nature which relate to religious practices, community and celebrations (a) What is the impact of religion and beliefs in the: · local community · wider area in and around Devon · diversity of the UK · global community (b) Why does hatred and persecution sometimes happen and what can be done to prevent it? (Focus on the Holocaust and subsequent genocides) (c) If religion did not exist who would miss it? Can religions and beliefs support people in difficult times? (Devon, 2014, p. 16)

The questions posed in this syllabus and the classroom enquiries proposed, explore fundamental questions of values as well as imparting knowledge. This kind of enquiry is required if students are to come to understand the diversity of contemporary society and to develop the dispositions needed to live responsibly in it.

6 Democratic Citizenship and Religious Education

Openness to others might be claimed as a fundamental capacity for living together democratically and further, for taking an active role as a citizen in a democracy. *The Council of Europe's Charter on Education for Democratic*

Citizenship and Human Rights Education has well-articulated the kind of education that needs to occur to educate future citizens, defining what is necessary to develop and foster students' participation in democratic engagement. Among a long list of what needs to be done, the Council of Europe expresses the importance of encouraging dialogue (Council of Europe, 2010, p. 9).

> Learning how to engage in dialogue with people whose values are different from one's own and to respect them is central to the democratic process and essential for the protection and strengthening of democracy and fostering a culture of human rights. (Council of Europe, 2016, p. 11)

The aim expressed above for education is crucial to combat a rising tide of popularism and nationalism in Europe. The Council expresses concern that "in Europe young people do not often have an opportunity to discuss controversial issues in school because they are seen as too challenging to teach, e.g. issues to do with extremism, gender violence, child abuse, or sexual orientation." They point out that lack of opportunities to engage in such discussions can be dangerous:

> Unable to voice their concerns, unaware of how others feel or left to rely on friends and social media for their information, young people can be frustrated or confused about some of the major issues which affect their communities and European society today. In the absence of help from school, they might have no reliable means of dealing with these issues constructively and no one to guide them. (ibid.)

Directly addressing responses to the radicalisation of young people, the publication goes on to state:

> Public concern arising in the aftermath of a number of high-profile incidents of violence and social disorder in different European countries has combined with new thinking in education for democracy and human rights to make the handling of controversial issues in schools a matter of educational urgency. (ibid.)

The Council points out that incidents such as the 2011 London riots, the 2011 Norwegian hate crimes and the Charlie Hebdo attack in Paris in 2015 have prompted a whole-scale review of the part played by schools in the moral and civic development of young people in these countries and across Europe.

Further, it approves of a shift in European policy on education for democracy and human rights "from reliance on text-book exercises and the acquisition of theoretical knowledge to an emphasis on active and participatory learning and engagement with 'real-life' issues" (ibid.).

> Learning how to engage in dialogue with people whose values are different from one's own and to respect them is central to the democratic process and essential for the protection and strengthening of democracy and fostering a culture of human rights. (Council of Europe, 2016, p. 11)

Allowing discussion of controversial issues and what might be considered 'extreme views' can enable students to change what they think and to develop their ideas and assimilate, imaginatively, something of another's experience (see Dewey, 1916, p. 8). Classroom discussion is important to enable individuals to develop understanding because it enables a safe space for unravelling possible implications of thought and action, for hearing the views of others, and for experiencing the reactions of others. As Nussbaum (2005) states:

> schools that help young people to speak in their own voice and to respect the voices of others will have done a great deal to produce thoughtful and potentially creative democratic citizens. (p. 6)

Religious education can contribute powerfully to the development of open-minded dispositions though the knowledge gained in studying world religions and through the exposure to different points of views on life issues and customs. This is particularly important in contemporary society.

> Cultivating our humanity in a complex interlocking world ... requires a great deal of knowledge that students in Europe and North America rarely got. It is easier to do this if one begins when children are young, so that they come to see the world – and their own nation itself – as complex and heterogeneous rather than as local and homogeneous. (Nussbaum, 2005, p. 6)

Nussbaum (2010) creates an argument for why democracy needs the humanities and why students in today's world need to understand how the global economy works, the history of the economy, and of national history and colonialism. She makes the following statement about the importance of religious education:

Equally crucial to the success of democracies in our world is the understanding of the world's, many religious traditions. There is no area (except,
perhaps, sexuality) where people are more likely to form demeaning stereotypes of the other that impede mutual respect and productive discussion. (Nussbaum, 2010, p. 83)

Nussbaum (2005) deplores the fact that religious education had been cut from
'a famous university,' which she did not name, because it was stated not to be
a 'core' humanity subject. RE is a core humanities subject, and we have seen
that the humanities can do 'imagination's heartwork' (Hogan, 2009) and foster
'education for sympathy.' Religious education can contribute much to this education for democracy, which is important.

Otherwise, young people are unlikely to be in a position to be challenged by what they see or hear ... to challenge expectations, to break
stereotypes, to change the ways in which persons apprehend the world.
(Greene, 1981, p. 123)

7   National Curriculum for Religious Education

While there is guidance from the Department for Education which governs
the English and Welsh curriculum, religious education is a compulsory subject but not a statutory National Curriculum subject, so not under the scrutiny
of Ofsted inspections. The syllabi are determined by local Standing Advisory
Councils on religious education (SACREs), independent bodies which consider
how religious education will be taught in schools under Local Authority juris-
diction. Academisation has taken many schools out of Local Authority juris-
diction. In fact, by August 2018, nearly three quarters of secondary schools and
three in ten primary schools had become academies and free schools. They
are obliged to teach religious education but do not have to follow the National
Curriculum. This leads to a variability of provision, in some cases little or no
provision, as well variability of syllabi. The aims of the national curriculum are
certainly in line with the potentiality and importance of RE as a curriculum
subject, one of these overarching aims being that

The national curriculum provides pupils with an introduction to the
essential knowledge they need to be educated citizens. It introduces
pupils to the best that has been thought and said and helps engender an
appreciation of human creativity and achievement. (DfE, 2014, 3.1)

More non statutory guidance was given in 2010 which underscores the key importance of the subject. RE, we are told

- *provokes challenging questions* about the meaning and purpose of life, beliefs, the self, issues of right and wrong, and what it means to be human. It develops pupils' knowledge and understanding of Christianity, other principal religions, and religious traditions that examine these questions, fostering personal reflection and spiritual development
- *encourages pupils to explore their own beliefs* (whether they are religious or non-religious), in the light of what they learn, as they examine issues of religious belief and faith and how these impact on personal, institutional and social ethics; and to express their responses. This also builds resilience to anti-democratic or extremist narratives
- *enables pupils to build their sense of identity and belonging,* which helps them flourish within their communities and as citizens in a diverse society
- *teaches pupils to develop respect for others,* including people with different faiths and beliefs, and helps to challenge prejudice
- *prompts pupils to consider their responsibilities* to themselves and to others, and to explore how they might contribute to their communities and to wider society. It encourages empathy, generosity and compassion. (DSCF, 2010, p. 8)

These descriptions of the potential of the subject underline why and how it is a key subject among the humanities, with its window into developing the sense of values and the dispositions necessary to be a citizen in a democratic society. However, there are two issues with the RE curriculum and provision as it currently stands. The first concerns the way in which religious education is conceived in the NC, with the status of Christianity as the primary religion in such a curriculum. Namely for the DfE, religious education "develops pupils' knowledge and understanding of Christianity, other principal religions, and religious traditions" (DfE, 2010, p. 8). Defining 'other religions' in relation to Christianity, signifying they are 'not-Christian,' perpetuates an otherness discourse that undermines the aim of promoting and developing 'inclusion.' This is a serious drawback to the underlying intentions of a curriculum that aims to promote sensitivity to diversity and openness to values that might be in conflict with personal beliefs.

The second concerns provision. If RE has the potential outlined in the chapter, it should be a compulsory subject and should be followed in all schools. Responding to these concerns as well as to a desire to re-evaluate RE the Commission on religious education (CoRE) took evidence over two years

(2016–2018) from parents, teachers, students and religious bodies, about how the subject of RE should be conceived, taught and monitored. The Commission has presented a National Plan for RE. Both the concerns noted above are addressed in its recommendations, which also point to a revitalising of the subject in its other recommendations. The Commission points first to a

> growing diversity of religions and beliefs that pupils today encounter, both in their locality and in the media. Second is the variable quality of RE experienced by pupils across the country. Third is the fact that the legal arrangements around RE are no longer working as more schools become academies. (CoRE, 2018, p. 3)

It is timely that the report identifies key areas for RE as a school subject. it should explore:

> the important role that religious and non-religious worldviews play in all human life. This is an essential area of study if pupils are to be well prepared for life in a world where controversy over such matters is pervasive and where many people lack the knowledge to make their own informed decisions. It is a subject for all pupils, whatever their own family background and personal beliefs and practices. (ibid.)

The Commission proposes that to reflect this new emphasis the subject should be called Religion and Worldviews, that a statutory national curriculum should apply to all schools, that the subject should be inspected and that training should be given to teachers to teach the new curriculum. These recommendations are sensible. To note that if philosophy of education were a core subject in teacher preparation programmes, such as the Postgraduate Certificate of. Education (PGCE) new teachers would at least be familiar with values education and with developing reflective activities. In many countries some form of civic education is a vehicle for promoting values and encouraging pupils to develop their ability to deliberate on moral matters. RE can provide this affordance in the English context. Clearly values underlie all aspects of school life. In some schools, there is a common understanding about the basis of these values in definable moral codes, such as in a faith school where there is accepted tradition and 'scripture.' In a secular school, a common understanding is not so tightly defined. Nevertheless, even in a faith school, there are many areas where value judgements are made, which are not clearly indicated by the underlying faith ethic, such as judgements about what is 'fair' in a particular situation, which may involve judgement in choosing one claim over another. Teachers

frequently have to make such judgements in particular situations. School policies, rules and regulations, may provide guidelines, for example, when dealing
with racist or bullying incidents, often based on the core value of 'respect,' but
this guidance cannot tell us what we *ought* to say and to do in response to a
particular situation. As a teacher, it is a matter of judgement how to mediate the policy. So, in acting and being in the classroom a teacher stands as a
moral example. For example, a teacher might punish a pupil who steals from
another pupil without much discussion; or the teacher might decide to talk
to the pupil, to get them to understand that what they had done was wrong.
Choosing how and when to have this discussion is also a matter of judgement.
Overall, then, a grounding in philosophy of education can support teachers in
all their roles in school and can certainly support RE teachers understanding in
their role.

8   Conclusion

Religious education is an important subject in creating a culture in which children can grow within the social, with knowledge of other religions and views,
which opens them to sets of values. But most importantly it provides the space
to discuss moral dilemmas within a context that is real, in the sense that arguments about abortion, same sex marriage, for example can be tackled from the
perspective of religious education in which a number of views can be heard.
The capacity for ethical deliberation can be fostered through dialogical pedagogy. At its best religious education is a subject which creates a space for the
development and maintenance of critical faculties and sympathetic imagination, particularly in its study of different religions and religious practices and
its promotion of dialogical pedagogy.

To promote socially democratic values is to draw on a view of what a democratic culture should be. Individuals are embedded in the social and the social
is made of, by and with them. In studying different religions and religious practices students will hopefully become open to the possibility of different ways
of conceiving the world. When they are encouraged to discuss ethical issues,
students are also given an opportunity to gain in understanding of their complexity. When well managed discussions take place on controversial issues in
the religious education classroom students have an opportunity to rehearse
arguments in safe situations. This depends however on well trained teachers
able to handle such discussions.

One of the hidden dimensions of religious education is that it is cultural
education and cultural education of the kind that covers the knowledge and

understanding, skills and capacities, defined in the religious education National Curriculum. Adding 'worldviews' to the title of the subject might go some way to acknowledging the role of culture in our lives, and particularly of the diverse nature of the cultures among which students in contemporary times live. It is a moot point then whether the word 'religious' becomes redundant. 'Worldviews education' might be a suitable change of name for a subject studied in school. 'Religious Education' can then be left to religious bodies as it is in some countries with strict separation between religion and state institutions.

Notes

1   See Hand (2016) for a more extended discussion.
2   See Dewey (1916, chapter 21) for an extended discussion of the topic.

References

Apple, M. W. (2005). Education, markets and an audit culture. *Critical Quarterly, 47*(2), 11–29.

Ball, S. (2000). Performativites and fabrications in the education economy: Towards the performative society. *Australian Educational Researcher, 27*(2), 1–23.

CoRE (Commision on Religious Education). (2018). *Religion and worldviews: The way forward. A national plan for RE. Final report.* Religious Education Council of England and Wales. Retrieved April 3, 2020, from https://www.religiouseducationcouncil.org.uk/wp-content/uploads/2017/05/Final-Report-of-the-Commission-on-RE.pdf

Council of Europe. (2010). *Charter on education for democratic citizenship and human rights education.* Strasbourg: Council of Europe Publishing.

Council of Europe. (2016). *Living with controversy. Teaching controversial issues through Education for Democratic Citizenship and Human Rights (EDC/HRE): Training pack for teachers.* Council of Europe Publishing.

DCSF. (2010). *Religion in schools, non-statutory guidance.* Retrieved November 19, 2019, from https://assets.publishing.service.gov.uk/government/uploads/system/uploads/attachment_data/file/190260/DCSF-00114-2010.pdf

Devon and Torbay Education Authority. (2014). *Agreed syllabus for religious education.* Retrieved November 19, 2019, from http://www.torbay.gov.uk/media/11247/torbay-agreed-syllabus-for-religious-education.pdf

Dewey, J. (1909). The moral principles in education. In J.-A. Boydston (Ed.), *The middle works of John Dewey, 1899–1924: 1907–1909, essays* (Vol. 4, pp. 67–292). Southern Illinois University Press.

Dewey, J. (1916). Democracy and education. In J.-A. Boydston (Ed.), *The middle works of John Dewey, 1899–1924* (Vol. 9). Southern Illinois University Press.

Dewey, J. (1922). Human nature and conduct. In J.-A. Boydston (Ed.), *The middle works of John Dewey, 1899–1924* (Vol. 9). Southern Illinois University Press.

Dewey, J. (1938). Experience and education. In J.-A. Boydston (Ed.), *The later works of John Dewey, 1925–1953* (Vol. 13, pp. 3–62). Southern Illinois University Press.

Dewey, J. (1939). *Freedom and culture.* In J.-A. Boydston (Ed.), *The later works of John Dewey, 1925–1953* (Vol. 13, pp. 64–188). Southern Illinois University Press.

DfE. (2014). *Statutory guidance: National curriculum in England: Framework for key stages 1 to 4 updated 2 December 2014.* Retrieved November 19, 2019, from https://www.gov.uk/government/publications/national-curriculum-in-england-framework-for-key-stages-1-to-4/the-national-curriculum-in-england-framework-for-key-stages-1-to-4

Greene, M. (1981). Aesthetic literacy in general education. In *80th yearbook of the national society for the study of education* (pp. 115–141). University of Chicago Press. Retrieved November 19, 2019, from http://www.scribd.com/doc/26620361/

Hand, M. (2016). Education for moral seriousness. In M. Hand & R. Davies (Eds.), *Education, ethics and experience: Essays in honour of Richard Pring* (pp. 48–61). Routledge.

Hogan, P. (2009). *The new significance of learning: Imagination's heartwork.* Routledge.

Keall, C. (2010). Exploring the nature and educational significance of Dewey's notion of growth. In *Panel: The centrality of Dewey's philosophy of growth: Clarifying Dewey's commitment to growth in ethics and education.* Society for the Advancement of American Philosophy, 37th Annual Meeting, University of North Carolina.

Nussbaum, M. C. (1997). *Cultivating humanity: A classical defense of reform in liberal education.* Harvard University Press.

Nussbaum, M. C. (2004). Liberal education and global community. *Liberal Education, 90*(1). Retrieved November 19, 2019, from https://www.aacu.org/publications-research/periodicals/liberal-education-global-community

Nussbaum, M. C. (2005, December). *Education for democratic citizenship.* Lecture given at the University of Athens. Retrieved November 19, 2019, from http://old.phs.uoa.gr/~ahatzis/Nussbaum1.pdf

Nussbaum, M. C. (2010). *Not for profit: why democracy needs the humanities.* Princeton University Press.

Oakeshott, M. (1989). Education: The engagement and its frustration. In T. Fuller (Ed.), *The voice of liberal learning* (pp. 63–94). Yale University Press. (Original work published 1972)

Pring, R. (1997). Educating persons. In R. Pring (Ed.) (2004), *Philosophy of education: Aims, theory, common sense and research* (pp. 26–41). Continuum.

Pring, R. (1999). Neglected educational aims: Moral seriousness and social commitment. In R. Marples (Ed.), *The aims of education* (pp. 157–172). Routledge.

Pring, R. (2013). *The life and death of secondary education for all.* Routledge.

CHAPTER 3

Education and Belonging to a Subject Matter

David Aldridge

Abstract

This chapter sets out a pedagogy of 'belonging' for religious education. It draws on the perspective of philosophical hermeneutics to elaborate the intentional relation of teacher, student and subject matter in the event of understanding. It is proposed that dialogue as an existential form has an educational significance that is further complicated when transferred into the 'ontic' situation in which the roles of teacher and student are formally assumed. The possibility of belonging as an educational 'ethic' is considered. Finally, it is acknowledged that the model of belonging applies as much to the encounter with the 'curriculum' as to the classroom situation, and some implications are drawn out for the 'questionability' of religious education.

Keywords

belonging – philosophical hermeneutics – instructional triangle – phenomenology – existential education – religious education

1   Introduction

This chapter attempts a theorisation of education as 'belonging' to a subject matter. By 'belonging' I do not mean that 'sense of belonging' as a dimension of religion that finds its way on to so many locally agreed syllabuses for religious education; rather I am referring to an existential relationship between teacher, student and their shared object of study. The chapter will concern itself primarily with a descriptive account of an existential possibility within all education but will turn in its closing paragraphs to a consideration of some implications for the curriculum subject *religious education*. The 'pedagogy of belonging' that is offered here will not serve, however, as a prescriptive methodology for how to go about religious education. It is not a case of 'applying' a general theory of education to a particular curriculum area; rather, the significance of thinking of education as an event of belonging is that we are reminded of the *question-ability* of religious education.

I approach this theorisation via hermeneutics, a disciplinary route that may be familiar to many teachers of religious education. I have engaged elsewhere in more detailed discussion of the different interpretations of 'hermeneutics' (Aldridge, 2011, 2013, 2015, 2018a). For the purposes of this chapter I will simply mention that the perspective adopted here draws from the 'philosophical hermeneutics' of Martin Heidegger and in particular Hans-Georg Gadamer, whose aim was to offer a phenomenological description of the event of understanding. To the extent that we agree that understanding plays a part in any educational event, we are justified in considering philosophical hermeneutics in our description of that event. This is worth saying in particular because recently the report of the Commission on Religious Education has been criticised for its implicit frame of 'hermeneuticism' (Hannam & Biesta, 2019; see also Biesta, 2016, 2017, for an elaboration of this critique). It will take far more space than I have in this chapter to respond in detail to this presentation of hermeneutics. Suffice to say for the time being that the version of philosophical hermeneutics sketched out here does not conform to the 'hermeneuticism' identified by Hannam and Biesta. Some rapprochement might be achieved by acknowledging that whereas Hannam and Biesta criticise the 'hermeneutical' frame for neglecting the *existential* dimensions of education, Gadamer and Heidegger criticised the hermeneutical tradition that preceded them for neglecting the *existential* dimensions of understanding, and that where Hannam and Biesta proceed by the somewhat unexpected move of decentring what they call 'understanding' within the educational event, philosophical hermeneutics proceeds by emphasising understanding's *existential* significance. What is picked out and emphasised in each case is (despite this initial semantic opposition) remarkably similar.[1]

2 The Educational Significance of Dialogue

A central pillar of Gadamer's philosophical hermeneutics is the 'dialogic' character of understanding (Gadamer, 2004; Aldridge, 2015, chapter 4). Even where he concerns himself in *Truth and Method* primarily with textual understanding, the dialogic model is more basic; the text itself is to be approached in an I-Thou relation (Gadamer, 2004, p. 363).[2] In educational literature, the Gadamerian insight into the dialogic nature of understanding has sometimes been taken to mean that we must have more classroom conversations in order to promote understanding (see Lefstein, 2006, for an account of the different ways that the idea of 'dialogue' is appropriated in education), but this misses the fact that (as Biesta points out in his own phenomenological, albeit not Gadamerian, approach to education), "dialogue is not to be understood as conversation but as an existential 'form'" (Biesta, 2017, p. 6). Essential to the dialogic nature of understanding is that it happens in an "in-between" that relates interpreter and what is understood (Gadamer, 2004, p. 295). Understanding is not the achievement of a subject acting on some object but confounds active and passive distinctions since it aims at "agreement concerning the subject matter" (p. 292). Gadamer contends that the route to understanding is through the question, and that understanding has a 'logic of question and answer' (Aldridge, 2013). An interpreter approaches a text from their own horizon of understanding, but does not limit the text's meaning in conformity to that horizon; rather the horizon itself is subject to transformation in response to "the experience of being pulled up short by the text" (Gadamer, 2004, p. 270). The 'question' the interpreter brings to the text is not one that can be thematised in propositional terms – it cannot be known or articulated ahead of an event of understanding – but rather emerges in that event. We say, Gadamer reminds us, "that a question too 'occurs' to us, that it 'arises' or 'presents itself' more than we raise or present it" (p. 360). Central to a phenomenological description of understanding is its event-like character: understanding transcends the efforts of the the one who understands; as Gadamer says, it *"happens to us over and above our wanting and doing"* (Gadamer, 2004, p. xxvi).

Gadamer is well known for his rehabilitation of 'prejudice' as an essential condition for understanding (Gadamer, 2004, pp. 273ff), where prejudices are the "biases of our openness to the world" (Gadamer, 1977, p. 9); the 'question' that gives shape to the subject matter then is better construed as an orientation in the being of the interpreter than as an epistemological construction. Hence the language of hermeneutics is often topological in character (Aldridge, 2015, pp. 3–4 and *passim*) and even the etymology of its central concern, 'understanding' (and in German 'Verständnis') carries this sense of standing in a related way to some subject matter. This disposition of openness – a "pure self-abandonment" (Gadamer, 1991, p. 39) – has an ethical dimension for Gadamer, because it requires allowing oneself "to be conducted by the subject matter" (Gadamer, 2004, p. 360). This can be better understood by comparing an authentic dialogue with what Gadamer calls its 'degenerate' forms, in which "one rigidifies oneself in ways that make one, precisely, unreachable by the other person" (Gadamer, 1991, p. 38) or in which the aim is to present oneself as "the one who knows" (Gadamer, 1991, p. 51). Authentic dialogue requires that a participant is open to transformation by what is to be understood or 'risks' the self (Gadamer, 2004, p. 399); in taking this risk the interpreter him or herself becomes questionable, in that he or she comes to stand in a new way towards the subject matter. The significance of the 'philosophical turn' in hermeneutics (see Aldridge, 2018a) is that an *epistemological* conception of understanding has been replaced by an *existential* challenge. What is gained in understanding (and it might be better here to think in terms of what is experienced or 'undergone' rather than what is gained) is not a matter of knowledge so much as a new orientation in and to the world.

Although a dialogic account of understanding breaks down the subject/object distinction, it does not simply replace a model of subjective agency with one of pure receptivity. Weinsheimer and Marshall comment that "participants in a conversation 'belong' to and with each other, 'belong' to and with the subject of their discussion, and mutually participate in the process which brings out the nature of that subject" (Weinsheimer & Marshall, 2004, p. xvi). They point out the connections between 'gehören' (to belong) and 'hören' (to hear, and also to obey) and the additional sense gehören has of granting what is due.[3] When two interlocutors understand each other, or when a reader understands a text, in each case the two are in a relationship of belonging with a third component, the subject matter (*die Sache*) that is at issue between them.

The disposition required for authentic understanding is a serious openness to the address of an interlocutor; an acceptance that they might make a claim on us or have something to teach us. Viewed in this light, the resemblance of the threefold hermeneutical 'belonging' (of the one who understands, their 'teacher' and their shared interest) to the instructional triangle – or what Standish (2014) has called the 'sacred' triangle of teacher, student and subject matter – is striking. This resemblance is what has led Gallagher to suggest that learning should be offered as the fundamental model for the hermeneutic situation (Gallagher, 1992, pp. 319–352) and leads me to the claim that what makes understanding authentically itself is its educational dimension (Aldridge, 2015, chapter 5). 'Agreement' (Einverständnis), which Gadamer describes as the aim of understanding, is a relation of intentional orientation towards a shared object. This shared orientation is quite compatible with disagreeing over the substantive claims that one's interlocutor makes about that subject; agreement is over what "comes to presence" (Wiensheimer & Marshall, 2004, p. xvi) as at issue between participants in dialogue.

I will round off this section by noting that belonging has so far in this chapter been offered descriptively as a condition of the existential state of understanding and does not imply any specific methodology; it is not as if there was a way of 'balancing' the relevant interests. Interlocutors can fall out of this state, and often do. They begin to speak at cross purposes or realise that they no longer have a shared interest. A moment of belonging might be more precarious or more committed, and a participant in dialogue (or a reader) might move in and out of belonging and into other conversational modes. Just as in the concrete context of conversation, there is no way of ensuring that a dialogue happens; coercion will not achieve that end, and one's interlocutor can always wander away.

3   Education as an Event of Belonging

So far, I have elaborated the educational dimension of hermeneutics but not the hermeneutical dimension of education, which will require complicating matters somewhat. Following Gadamer (2001), the discussion of education so far has begun from the context of self-education, and the title of 'teacher' has been accorded in terms of what has been given and received in the dialogic exchange rather than in terms of a fixed role. In the context of self-education, an interpreter approaches a text as its student and may depart again having decided that they have all they need from this dialogue, or in discovering that it no longer 'speaks' to them. In a dialogue between two participants there is always the possibility that each will learn from the other, even if it is not necessary that this relationship is equal (in the event, one's insight may prove more enriching to the other than the other way round). The aims of a dialogue emerge along with its subject matter; the dialogue continues for as long as the participants are prepared to be governed by the shared subject matter and follow it as it is disclosed for them.

Adopting a distinction offered by Heidegger (1962), we could say that the teacher/student roles we have so far discussed are *ontological* rather than *ontic*: that is, I have considered them as existential possibilities rather than concrete social or institutional roles, in which one participant (a teacher) has the task of initiating a particular kind of dialogic situation. The existential roles of teacher, student and subject matter do not map neatly on to their apparently corresponding institutional roles. Gallagher has made a significant contribution to understanding the situation by pointing out the multiplication of dialogues involved even in a simplified 'classroom' context of teacher, single student and the 'subject matter' to be taught (to say nothing of what happens when this constellation is multiplied across a classroom full of students)

> Learning requires (a) a dialogue or circulating relationship between an individual learner's fore-structure and the subject matter; and (b) a dialogue between the teacher's understanding and the pedagogical presentation. These two kinds of dialogue or interchanges are not unrelated; as

parts, they enter into a third dialectical interchange which constitutes the whole of the classroom situation – (c) the give and take of discussion, the interchange of interpretations between teacher and student. (Gallagher, 1992, p. 74)

Gallagher has not drawn out the full implications of this observation. I have discussed them in more detail elsewhere (Aldridge, 2015, chapter 4) and will offer only a brief summary here. What has intruded into the 'educational' relation that was not yet at play in the dialogic situation discussed in the previous section is some curriculum, scheme, or formal accountability structure which has determined or prescribed an object of study. I prefer to retain the term 'subject matter' for Gadamer's ontologically significant use of *die Sache;* Gallagher's phrase 'subject matter' in the quotation above does not refer to this; in fact, each of the three separate dialogic interactions, following the description I have offered above, will have its own emergent subject matter in its own possible relation of belonging.

Since these are not three unconnected dialogues, there is the possibility of a further moment of belonging, in which some mutual understanding occurs and each of the three hermeneutic conversations becomes intentionally oriented to the same emergent subject matter; it is this unity that we might say a pedagogy of belonging 'aims' at. The possibility of reaching this moment of belonging seems ever more precarious, since it is accompanied by a multiplication of the ways that teacher and student might come to talk at cross purposes, or might rigidify themselves in relation to the claims made on them by the object of study.

Whereas the object of study is determinate (it is prescribed by a curriculum or scheme), no-one can know what will come out of the student's encounter with it. Interpreting Gadamer for education, Paul Fairfield argues that "a genuine conversation is never the one we wanted to conduct" (Fairfield, 2011, p. 79). It is for this reason that I have written that *aiming* for educational belonging is in tension with following a curriculum or scheme (Aldridge, 2013), and that a moment of belonging might be something that emerges in the classroom *in spite of* our best 'educational' efforts (Aldridge, 2018a). Institutional demands of planning and accountability require that a teacher knows above all where students need to be next in their learning and how to get them there. Yet most teachers have experienced a moment where they have felt that a dialogue was educationally valuable but was taking up too much time and diverging too far from the specification, and have thus uttered the words 'let's move on' (feeling at the same time that what was actually happening was not 'moving on' but actually an interruption of some significant movement by a predetermined scheme). Conceding that such instances might be rare in our experience does not undermine their importance as moments where the foreclosure of an existential possibility is foregrounded in a concrete conversation. The significance of the *existential* dialogue I have discussed above is that it is implicated in all possible movements of understanding, not only those concrete spoken situations; 'belonging' is not therefore normally subject to direct observation by the teacher and may well be subject to numerous unseen frustrations in the encounter with a prescriptive curriculum.

No predetermined mastery of the demands of the curriculum or exertion of institutional authority can prevent a student from 'wandering away' from dialogue; an encounter with a curriculum that already 'knows' full well what he or she requires might well be what leads a child to "go missing" (existentially speaking) from the classroom (Hannam, 2019, p. 63). A further indicator of the indeterminacy of what is at stake between teachers and students is that the teachers must become learners even in order to fulfil their institutional duties: they must respond in a 'to and fro' courtship to the engagement of the student with what is taught, or their push back, and must amend their approach to accommodate a student's disclosure of sensibilities, inclinations, aversions and barriers, so many of which are affective and (despite what the learning scientists would have us think) *existential* – or, as I have written elsewhere, *carnal* (Aldridge, 2019) – rather than cognitive. Teachers are – of course – not helpless in this endeavour; they have resources of human expertise that are better captured in the idea of pedagogical tact than of scientific method; but they cannot plan or prepare for belonging in advance of these disclosures.

4   Belonging as an Educational Ethic?

Before I discuss some implications for the relation of religion and education, I want to consider some objections that might be raised to the description I have offered. A general criticism of the phenomenological approach I have employed might be that I have not argued for the importance of belonging in education so much as described it into existence. The analysis ultimately stands or falls on its capacity to shed light on that tension in the lived experience of the teacher between the moment of belonging and the curriculum or scheme. Additional recognition might be found from teachers and scholars of religious education in the UK familiar with Grimmitt's (1987) distinction between 'learning about' and 'learning from' and the questions that have been asked since its introduction about how to 'balance' the demands of religious content and the need for the student to relate it to their own experience.

I have written that the emphasis on *both* learning about *and* learning from is an educational insight whose significance extends beyond religious education (Aldridge, 2011, 2015). Both the horizon of the student and the horizon of the object of study are accommodated in the moment of belonging, but no algorithm can be offered for weighing up their relative demands; a related orientation (the 'fusion of horizons') is precisely what is achieved or undergone in the moment of belonging.

To the concern that 'hearkening' or allowing oneself to be conducted by the subject matter means yielding uncritically to a text or worldview that might be distorting or harmful, I can only reiterate my claim that one can learn from a text without agreeing with its substantive claims: "If a prejudice becomes questionable in view of what another person or a text says to us, this does not mean that it is simply set aside and the text or the other person accepted as valid in its place ... In fact our own prejudice is properly brought into play by being put at risk" (Gadamer, 2004, pp. 298–299). It might be objected that education might have a more modest aim than is suggested here, and that it need not and ought not to seek always to 'transform' or 'reorient' but might simply aim at knowledge. My response would begin with Gadamer's insight that the separate movements of medieval hermeneutics – the *subtilitas intelligendi* and the *subtilitas applicandi* – are one, and that there is no understanding without application (Aldridge, 2011, 2015); thus there is no possibility of separating out the 'gaining' of knowledge from taking a stance on it. Because dialogue is this site of ongoing disclosure and orientation to the world, Gadamer thinks in terms of the 'happening of truth' rather than the acquisition of knowledge. Even if it is not the case that education conceived as 'belonging' is not concerned at all with knowledge, at least it can be emphasised that any knowledge gained through understanding has its existential component: it is inseparable from this new orientation of the being of the one that understands (see Aldridge, 2018b, for an elaboration of this claim). This is not to say that an educator cannot *aim* only at knowledge without consideration for how it will 'take' in the lived experience of the student; but what will subsequently befall the student in existential terms is largely beyond their capacity to predict or control.

To the charge that although I have claimed that belonging is not prescriptive, I have nevertheless offered an educational 'ideal,' I agree that I am more susceptible. Fairfield implies an ethic for belonging, I think, when he claims that, "Insofar as anyone or anything presides over the conversation in an educational setting, it is the subject matter itself that does so, the text, the problem, or question that orients the discussion, rather than any particular participant, be it professor or student" (Fairfield, 2011, p. 79). There seems to be an ethical significance to acknowledging that there could also be moments of 'partial belonging,' such as when a teacher and a student become complicit in devoting themselves to learning the requirements of an exam specification rather than heeding the claim of the object of study to be explored on its own terms; here each 'belongs' to the other in their mutual decision to excel in a certain sort of explication that (to appropriate some words of Biesta's that are connected in spirit) "can never replace the existential challenge and can sometimes actually become an excuse for not having to engage with it" (Biesta, 2017, p. 13). This two-sided belonging excludes the subject matter, and thus retreats from the existential possibility that Fairfield offers. I appreciate that there are numerous motivations and pressures in play in educational contexts, and do not mean to condemn a teacher (no less a student) who at any given moment takes a stance other than Fairfield's, only to point out that this indeed what they have done – taken a stance on the task of education.

5   The Questionability of Religious Education

It should perhaps be becoming clear to the reader that this dialogic model of education does not only apply to classroom discourse (Pinar, 2012, p. 56), and that the existential challenge of belonging applies as much to those broader decisions we might make about where to direct students' attention in our educational endeavours. Although I have pointed out that belonging in the classroom situation is in tension with a sense of progression through some predetermined scheme, education in its 'ontic' form cannot do without its 'curriculum' in the sense that educators must begin their efforts from "a selection that represents what a community believes is worthwhile" (Applebee, 1996, p. 42). This selection must also be viewed hermeneutically; as the curriculum theorist William Pinar has argued, teachers as professionals also participate in a "complicated conversation that is curriculum" (ibid). One characteristic of dialogue discussed above is that its aims cannot be given in advance but emerge along with the subject matter. An implication of this is that no once and for all justification can be given for offering any particular object of study or collection of curriculum objects. Acknowledging that participation in curriculum is a dialogic process means acknowledging that the very justifications we offer for the value of a given curriculum object can come into question in the encounter between teacher and student.

This is an insight that applies as much to any curriculum area as to religious education, but it is worth emphasising for the sake of scholarship that seeks to move from a general account of education to the particular discussion of what we might 'make' of religious education. Even calls for a radical re-evaluation of what we mean by religion (see Biesta & Hannam, 2016; Hannam, 2018) appear to accept the study of religion within a discrete curriculum area as a brute fact. It is a given that the curriculum discussion of religious education in England and Wales is already underway, but this dialogue has emerged according to a very particular and contingent history which has given it its shape; we do not have to look very far in our academic scholarship to see that things might have been otherwise, and that religion might not in other circumstances have been granted this discrete place on the curriculum at all. This foregrounds the questionability of what is it that we value when we offer religious education to the student (or, as I am currently inclined to put the question when speaking with religious education practitioners: what do we love when we love our subject?). It is increasingly popular to emphasise the intrinsic value of the 'disciplines' that traditionally have a voice in curriculum creation in religious education (see Kueh, 2017; Chater, 2020). I would certainly want to emphasise the role of that disciplinary voice in the moment of belonging; it is within a particular (complex, and contested) disciplinary history that the subject area of religious education has gathered its 'objects' (see Aldridge, 2015, chapter 1), and it is in light of their own disciplinary awareness that teachers make judgements about the address a given curriculum object might make to a student. But emphasising the close entanglement of discipline and curriculum object is at odds with an attempt to establish one academic discipline (or group of disciplines) as a fixed point from which a selection of curriculum objects might be justified; rather, the disciplinary approach becomes questionable *along with* the curriculum object whose significance it serves to constitute.

The challenge of the questionability of religious education becomes more urgent, rather than less, in light of moves to acknowledge the 'theological' significance of education 'writ large.' For example, religious educators might see some affinity between the employment of the Levinasian concepts of transcendence and revelation in Biesta's general account of education and the particular theological emphasis of their own subject area (see Biesta, 2017). The same might apply to Biesta's identification of 'existential challenge' as definitive of the educational task (see Biesta, 2017). But the implication of such bids from religion or the existential for the *whole* curriculum is that it is then more, rather than less, difficult to use the same arguments as a justification for giving over discrete curriculum space to a particular set of 'religious' or existential objects.

A pedagogy of belonging calls us to continually revise our provisional stance on these considerations in response to an existential challenge which arises from the direction of the student in their encounter with the curriculum object; this is a challenge which can appear as 'disengagement' but is actually a call to teach, and is concretely embodied in the moment when a student says, "So what?"

Notes

1   As I try to make clear in this chapter, there are resources within the hermeneutical tradition that provide support for the concerns Hannam and Biesta express about the Commission's report (CoRE, 2018).
2   See Aldridge (2015, pp. 87–89) and Gallagher (1992, pp. 320–331) for further discussion of the debate around textual versus dialogic priority in Gadamer.
3   See also Caputo (1983) for an extended discussion of the significance of 'belonging' to the subject matter.

References

Aldridge, D. (2011). What is religious education all about? A hermeneutic reappraisal. *Journal of Beliefs and Values, 32*(1), 33–45.

Aldridge, D. (2013). The logical priority of the question: R.G. Collingwood, philosophical hermeneutics and enquiry-based learning. *Journal of Philosophy of Education, 47*(1), 71–85.

Aldridge, D. (2015). *A hermeneutics of religious education*. Bloomsbury.

Aldridge, D. (2018a). Religious education's double hermeneutic. *British Journal of Religious Education, 40*(3), 245–256.

Aldridge, D. (2018b). Cheating education and the insertion of knowledge. *Educational Theory, 68*(6), 609–624

Aldridge, D. (2019). Education's love triangle. *Journal of Philosophy of Education, 53*(3), 531–546.

Applebee, A. N. (1996). *Curriculum as conversation: Transforming traditions of teaching and learning*. University of Chicago Press.

Biesta, G. (2016). The rediscovery of teaching: On robot vacuum cleaners, non-egological education and the limits of the hermeneutical worldview. *Educational Philosophy and Theory, 48*(4), 374–392.

Biesta, G. (2017). *The rediscovery of teaching*. Routledge.

Biesta, G., & Hannam, P. (2016). Religious education and the return of the teacher. *Religious Education, 111*(3), 293–242.

Caputo, J. (1983). The thought of being and the conversation of mankind: The case of Heidegger and Rorty. *The Review of Metaphysics, 36*(3), 661–85.

Chater, M. (2020). *Reforming RE. Power and knowledge in a worldviews curriculum.* John Catt.

CoRE (Commision on Religious Education). (2018). *Religion and worldviews: The way forward. A national plan for RE. Final report.* Religious Education Council of England and Wales. Retrieved April 3, 2020, from https://www.religiouseducationcouncil.org.uk/wp-content/uploads/2017/05/Final-Report-of-the-Commission-on-RE.pdf

Fairfield, P. (2011). Dialogue in the classroom. In P. Fairfield (Ed.), *Education, dialogue and hermeneutics* (pp. 77–90). Continuum.

Gadamer, H.-G. (1977). *Philosophical hermeneutics* (D. Linge, Trans.). University of California Press.

Gadamer, H.-G. (1991). *Plato's dialectical ethics* (R. M. Wallace, Trans.). Yale University Press.

Gadamer, H.-G. (2001). Education is self-education. *Journal of Philosophy of Education, 35*(4), 529–538.

Gadamer, H.-G. (2004). *Truth and method* (J. Weinsheimer & D. G. Marshall, Trans.). Continuum.

Gallagher, S. (1992). *Hermeneutics and education.* State University of New York Press.

Grimmitt, M. (1987). *Religious education and human development.* McCrimmon.

Hannam, P. (2018). *Religious education and the public sphere.* Routledge.

Hannam, P., & Biesta, G. (2019). Religious education, a matter of understanding? Reflections on the final report of the Commission on Religious Education. *Journal of Beliefs and Values, 40*(1), 55–63.

Heidegger, M. (1962). *Being and time* (J. Macquarrie & E. Robinson, Trans.). Blackwell.

Kueh, R. (2017). Religious education and the 'knowledge problem.' In M. Castelli & M. Chapter (Eds.), *We need to talk about religious education* (pp. 53–70). Jessica Kingsley.

Lefstein, A. (2006). *Dialogue in schools: Towards a pragmatic approach.* Working Papers in Urban Language and Literacy. King's College London.

Pinar, W. (2012). *What is curriculum theory?* Routledge.

Standish, P. (2014). Impudent practices. *Ethics and Education, 40*(3), 245–256.

Weinsheimer, J., & Marshall, D. G. (2004). Translators' preface. In H.-G. Gadamer (Ed.), *Truth and method* (J. Weinsheimer & D. G. Marshall, Trans.) (pp. xi–xix). Continuum.

CHAPTER 4

Religion, Reductionism and Pedagogical Reduction

David Lewin

Abstract

This chapter addresses some theoretical questions around educational representation. How are we to encourage others to develop a rich understanding of religion(s)? What is involved in the selections and simplifications of religious traditions for educational purposes, and how are these generalisations and constructions justified? This chapter addresses these questions by developing and applying a theory of *pedagogical reduction*. I contrast the educationally constructive notion of pedagogical reduction to what is often taken to be problematic in understanding religion, namely *reductionism*. I propose that understanding religion entails the complex pedagogical practices of the give and take of pedagogical reduction.

Keywords

pedagogical reduction – reductionism – representation – world religions paradigm – pedagogical tact

1   Introduction

This chapter addresses some theoretical questions around the educational representation of religion in general and religions in particular. How are we to encourage others to develop a rich understanding of the concept of religion? How ought we to teach children about complex and diverse religious traditions in an age of religious pluralism and multiculturalism as well as conflict and misrepresentation (Masuzawa, 2005)? What is involved in the selections and simplifications of religious traditions for educational purposes and how do these generalisations rely on a general construction of religion? How are those selections, simplifications and constructions justified? Can reductive representations such as the 'World Religions Paradigm' (Cotter & Robertson, 2016) really offer a balanced view of our diverse religious experiences and

© DAVID LEWIN, 2021 | DOI: 10.1163/9789004446397_005

traditions, or do they distort and misrepresent? This chapter addresses these questions by developing and applying a theory of pedagogical reduction. I contrast the educationally constructive notion of pedagogical reduction to what is often taken to be a problematic approach to understanding religion, namely *reductionism*. How can an educationally constructive reduction deal with the dangers of reductionism? My argument moves through four main steps. First, I define reductionism in general and raise the question of how much reduction is too much when it comes to representing religion. Second, I elaborate the concept of the *pedagogical reduction* which, in short, concerns the way complex and wide-ranging phenomena are represented in simple forms for educational purposes. This is followed by an exploration of how Religious Education and Religious Studies exhibit particular kinds of tension and ambivalence in relation to pedagogical reduction, finally leading to some theoretical and practical considerations around how pedagogical reductions require the development of certain educational dispositions, specifically illustrated through the notion of pedagogical tact.

2 Reductionism

In the field of Religious Studies, reductionism has a long and chequered history (Idinopulos & Yonan, 1993; Segal, 1983). We can broadly characterise reductive theories of religion as displaying two explanatory tendencies: naturalistic and cultural reductionism (Flood, 2011). Both natural and cultural theorising reduce religious phenomena and experience by imposing interpretive frames, the former through explaining phenomena in terms of more basic physical structures (e.g. neurochemistry), the latter in terms of more basic structures of power (e.g. Marxian critique). There are no conclusive means of determining whether, and to what extent, interpretive frames reveal or conceal. In general, it seems likely that the act of understanding through reductive framing of phenomena is ambivalent, and so we might acknowledge that, as Heidegger put it, every revealing is a concealing (Heidegger, 1977). From this perspective, neurochemical or Marxist interpretations of religious experiences and attitudes are not simply true or false but show something while obscuring something else. Acknowledging that we find ourselves within a hermeneutic circle, means that our interpretations and understandings are always provisional: they show something without every exhausting what can be shown.

Yet reductionism becomes problematic when certain phenomena (e.g., consciousness; religious experience; free will) are thought to be conclusively explained as epiphenomena: that the reality of the phenomena can be sufficiently explained by reference to basic constituents (e.g. neurochemistry or hegemony) and that the lived experience is illusory (Gallagher, 2006) or false consciousness. This kind of reductionism does not let the phenomena show itself as itself and has been roundly criticised by theorists particularly within phenomenology and hermeneutics (e.g. Gallagher, 2018; Dreyfus, 1992). In the context of Religious Education and Religious Studies,[1] reductionism is evident in the arguably hegemonic dominance of what is known as the 'World Religions Paradigm' (WRP); a way of interpreting, representing and teaching religion that emerged in the 1960's, particularly in the United Kingdom. This WRP has been characterised by Cotter and Robertson as follows:

> The WRP typically includes 'the Big Five' (where does that term come from?) of Christianity, Islam, Judaism, Hinduism and Buddhism – and moreover almost always presented in that Abrahamocentric order – increasingly with additional 'catch-all' categories such as 'indigenous religions' or 'new religions' included. (Cotter & Robertson, 2016, p. 2)

The WRP allows for a relatively systematic representation of religion in the face of religious pluralism and multiculturalism. But what are the benefits and what the costs of this systematic representation? Scholars of Religious Studies have sought ways to develop broader understandings of diverse religious traditions expanding the discipline of Religious Studies well beyond the constraints of (confessional) Theology (Smart, 1996). Some have interpreted the WRP as broadening the previously hegemonic and univocal confessional approach taken by religious educators. These changes had considerable influence over how schools, colleges and universities represent diverse religious traditions within Religious Education and Religious Studies. More recently, others have argued that understanding religion in contemporary RE and RS often pays the price of being excessive reductive: teachers of RE and RS tend to interpret and represent complex and diverse traditions through the narrow lenses derived from, most often, Western Protestant Christian religion (Smith, 1978; Harvey, 2013). In short, WRP has been criticised as too reductionistic (Owen, 2011). And yet, scholars have pointed to the necessity for something akin to a world religions approach, but that this should not be undertaken uncritically (Cotter & Robertson, 2016). So, although Cotter and Robertson's book presents a range of criticisms levelled at the WRP itself as being hegemonic and reductive, it also acknowledges the practical necessity for representation. From a hermeneutic perspective, these competing views of the WRP tell us something about the rich and complex field of religion, without exhausting the subject.

In what follows I develop something like this latter view that, although representation is always partial, it is educationally vital and constructive. This educationally constructive pedagogical reduction should not, I suggest, be confused with reductionism. The distinction I wish to make is between a problematic *reductionism* which sees the representation of phenomena as necessary and sufficient for complete understanding, and a *pedagogical reduction* which is necessary but never sufficient. I believe that this distinction is particularly significant for RE/RS because the 'content' of RE/RS can often be oriented to something that ostensibly and explicitly exceeds representation. Indeed, scholars and practitioners of religion regard the notion of representation with a degree of ambivalence not found in all curricula domains.[2] This means that in RE/RS educators are especially concerned to avoid the pitfalls of reductionism, but without a clear sense of what and how to reduce their subject matter in educational ways without falling into reductionism which, by definition cannot be very educational. Although I do not claim to offer substantive criteria for distinguishing reductionism and pedagogical reduction, my argument unfolds some conceptual resources designed to help us to reflect on, articulate, and usefully enact this distinction (see also Lewin, 2020).

3   Pedagogical Reduction

One of the fundamental questions educators must consider is one of educational representation: how is the complexity of things to be made understandable to the next generation? Much of what we call education, that is, the acts of presenting and representing the world,[3] could be boiled down to the efforts to draw the attention of students to particular things, efforts which involve various forms of selection and simplification aimed, generally speaking, towards something rather mysterious, even miraculous[4]: namely 'understanding.'

These efforts to draw attention include activities such as selecting, simplifying, generalising, and using examples, which taken together are directed towards the creation of conditions for learning, development or growth. This variety of activities undertaken to represent the complexity of the world for educational purposes is here referred to as *pedagogical reduction*. So, reduction refers to the activities that 'reduce' (the 'how') but also to the resulting representations that might be called 'reductions' (the 'what'), for instance, the summary of a subject field into a textbook chapter. Although the processes of pedagogical reduction are activities that most, if not all, educators would recognise, there is relatively little theory of educational representation and reduction among Anglo-American educational theorists.[5] Considerations of the similar Germanic notion of 'didactic reduction' (*Didaktische Reduktion*) seem to be largely absent within Anglo-American educational theory perhaps because of the paternalistic connotations of 'didactics.' Although criticisms of the particular forms that pedagogical reductions take are appropriate, my approach here affirms the intrinsic value of examining the general structure of pedagogical reduction (Lewin, 2019). I seek to explore the concept of pedagogical(-didactical) reduction primarily in descriptive terms, that is, without immediately engaging in normative critiques of the validity of certain reductions. This is not meant to suggest that such critiques are not significant or worthwhile. On the contrary, critical theory is of vital significance to educational representation. But I suggest that before (or perhaps after) critique (see Vlieghe & Zamojski, 2019), we must have some notion of what it is we wish to critique.

If it is true that most educators recognise selection, simplification and so on, why does it matter if they lack a theory? As already suggested, it is not the case that theoretical discourse around pedagogical representation is entirely lacking, but that such theory tends to move directly to forms of critique: progressive and critical pedagogues are prone to focus analysis on normative questions of the failures of representation, from critical analysis of whose interests govern pedagogical representations, to how we should avoid constructing inauthentic educational realities disconnected from a putative real world. For instance, a hermeneutics of suspicion is applied to the interests that govern the structure and content of textbooks (Apple, 2014). Although critical attitudes are often appropriate, especially where the education of adults is involved, I argue that the impact of the absence of a more general theory of pedagogical reduction is that insufficient attention is paid to the appropriate nature and scope of pedagogical reduction. In other words, while critics are apt to point out that the content of a particular curriculum is complex and contested, often representing unacknowledged and prejudiced canonical interests, there is seldom an explicit recognition and justification of the need for pedagogical reduction *per se*.

This leaves educators with, so to speak, one arm tied behind their backs: they must consider pedagogical relations and processes, attempting as they do to create conditions for growth, but are unsure of how the restrictions (and reductions) that constitute educational 'spaces' can make positive contributions to the construction of those conditions. Moreover, there are the twin pressures of progressive education commanding educators to abandon the inauthentic or reduced forms, versus so-called traditional educators demanding a return to the whole within sufficient consciousness concerning whose interests govern that whole. Understanding pedagogical practices of (both literally and metaphorically) fencing off experiences in children's nurseries, for instance, or understanding the need to 'suspend' the temporalities of instrumentalism within the school (Masschelein & Simons, 2013), can help educators to theorise as well as to practice pedagogical reduction well. I wish to highlight the specifically *educational* questions of pedagogical reduction that I believe are primary. Only in the wake of such a general analysis (i.e. general didactics) are we in a position to engage in critique of the particular forms (i.e., special didactics).

Although the concept of reduction describes conditions of constraint – the limiting structures of selection and simplification, as well as the literal constraints of space and time that classrooms and timetables bring about – it is also generative or productive, since these constraining conditions simultaneously bring things into view. To borrow a metaphor from Robert Macfarlane, the reduction is understood less as a perimeter that restricts, "but an aperture: a space through which the world can be seen" (Shepherd, 2014, p. xiii). The term is used both as a verb (to reduce something by making it smaller or simpler) and as a noun (the object, space or moment that has been reduced). Containing the verb stem *educe* which literally means to "draw out, extract; branch out" (Online Etymology Dictionary, 2019), the etymology refers to the idea of "bringing back, or restoring," employing *ducere*, meaning "bring, or lead out." Thus, to *reduce*, to *educe* and to *educate*, all connote drawing or bringing something out. By drawing attention, education is a generative reduction of the world which draws out through constraint.

This emphasises the verbal process, but I also want to keep in mind that reduction is a helpful term for the objects that result from the process. Textbooks are probably the paradigmatic form of the pedagogical reduction, since it is here that a subject field is represented in condensed form and simplified for the purposes of developing an understanding of a field. It is not only through texts and images that are representations deployed. Museums, galleries and exhibitions use light and space in certain ways, drawing attention to certain things with pedagogical intention; children's toys often present elements of the world in miniature, again with at least partial pedagogical or developmental interests; children's moral tales are often designed to simplify complex ethical or social dilemmas, or to sanitise darker instincts with formative influence in mind (Lewin, 2020). These and other forms of intentional reduction are everywhere in education. Two developed examples will suffice: one unconventional, the child's balance bike, and a second more conventional, the textbook.

Balance bikes are typically small bikes without gears, pedals, and often brakes and have become very popular in recent years. Although something like the balance bike has existed nearly as long as cycling itself, the modern form of the balance bike has become popular as the process of learning to ride a bike has evolved. Learning to ride is often understood to build upon the fundamental skills of balance and steering. Once they are developed, then other skills like pedalling, braking, and gears, can become the focus. Prior to the development of the balance bike, stabilisers (also known as training wheels) were (and still are) commonly used, though increasingly it is recognised that to remove the element of balance from the early stages of learning to ride, is counterproductive (Becker & Jenny, 2017; Rochmann, 2011). Clearly both kinds of training bike embody pedagogical reduction, but the use of stabilisers is arguably not as effective as using a balance bike for the intended purpose (learning to ride a bike). In either case, these bikes are used to simplify by breaking down a complex activity into constituent parts that are presented in a staged manner.

It is more common to recognise the pedagogical representations and reductions of more 'bookish' forms of knowledge. For instance, Daniel Tröhler distinguishes between a kind of academic or research knowledge, from pedagogical knowledge. Research knowledge is generated by questioning existing knowledge using verifiable scientific methods, resulting in new, but still provisional knowledge. This kind of knowledge is contrasted with pedagogical knowledge whose chief characteristic is to be "combined, arranged and structured for the purpose of effective teaching" (Tröhler, 2008, p. 79). The presentation of pedagogical knowledge, often in textbook form, follows certain principles: the knowledge is stable, not provisional or contested; exceptions and contradictions are avoided; elements are presented in discrete parts or units; the presentation itself is often attractive or entertaining in some way. In summary, this involves "[s]election, condensation, composition, didactical structuring and streamlining for classroom instruction" (Tröhler, 2008, p. 79).

This distinction between research and pedagogical knowledge can be overstated: one must keep in mind that as soon as one attempts to communicate research findings in journal articles and 'academic' texts, one is (one hopes!) thinking about how to clearly and persuasively present an argument, and so questions of pedagogical representation attend any consideration of research 'knowledge exchange.' Conversely, pedagogical knowledge is not disconnected from research knowledge as though it is only concerned with the practicalities of effective communication: even pedagogical knowledge is about something actual. Nevertheless, the distinction is useful and visible in all sorts of contexts. Tröhler goes on to discuss the Heidelberg Catechism, a Protestant confessional document published a few decades after Luther's publication of the 95 theses, as "a prime example of an educational work or 'textbook' that treats knowledge pedagogically" (Tröhler, 2008, p. 81), and which illustrates so well the principles of pedagogical reduction particularly in reference to Religious Education.

Published in 1563, the Heidelberg Catechism is said to have been the most popular text of the sixteenth century, at least in the Western World (Tröhler, 2008, p. 81). Whether the primary intentions of its authors were pedagogical or ecumenical (and how far these intentions can be disentangled) is debatable (Dreyer, 2014; Bierma, 2005). But this Lutheran catechetical form – a series of questions with orthodox responses – captures the elements of pedagogical reduction: it ensures some general theological consistency in a volatile age of reformation and counter-reformation. The way that the Canadian Reformed Theological Seminary website presents this Catechism is instructive:

> The Catechism summarizes the major teachings of Holy Scripture in one hundred and twenty-nine memorable questions and answers. Simple yet profound, as well as concise yet sufficient, the Catechism has been appreciated by young and old alike as one of the most clear, helpful and comforting guides into all the spiritual treasures of the holy gospel. (An Ageless Summary of an Everlasting Comfort, 2019)

The Catechism has been represented in so many visual forms because it distils the essence of the gospel, it elides theological controversies, and it attempts to meet the student where he or she is through forming questions that, it is supposed, exist within the reader. Note the surprising claim that the Catechism is 'sufficient.' As discussed earlier, the definition of a problematic kind of reductionism is related to the fact that the representation is thought to be sufficient. In general, sufficiency refers to the idea that nothing else is required, that the account is complete. Could the Heidelberg Catechism really be sufficient? It is clear that reduction is not a substitute for the Bible: "[T[he Catechism is not a replacement for Scripture. It is meant to lead you deeper into the Word of God, not draw you away from it" (An Ageless Summary of an Everlasting Comfort, 2019). One might argue that its sufficiency is not meant literally, but pedagogically: the statement of sufficiency might be intended to draw attention to the Catechism as a first step along a path that ultimately leads to Scripture itself. The Catechism is not Scripture but is something like a pedagogical representation and reduction of it. This raises the thorny issue of the relation between the representation and what is represented, not only in RE, but generally. After all, is not the reductive model of the physical brain only that: a model rather than the thing itself? We are always working within the realm of representation, it would seem. It would also seem that the initial definitions of reductionism require further analysis.

A wider discussion of the nature of scientific reductionism is beyond my scope, but the form of the Heidelberg Catechism suggests that something pedagogical is intended here: that Scripture is itself complex, open to varied interpretation (risking heresy), and perhaps inaccessible to some. But with the idea of making a pedagogical reduction of Scripture, we are faced with tensions: does the reduction risk *mis*representation? Is it not preferable to present students with the uninterpreted 'primary texts'? Are representations really necessary? Aren't textbook reductions too often used to elide or defer the real encounter with the substance of the curriculum perhaps because we think too little of the students, or too much of ourselves? Don't textbooks create a false scholastic (or educational) reality (Masschelein & Simons, 2013), what progressive educators might decry as an inauthentic educational space? More dramatically, don't textbooks occasionally get things quite wrong, or often intentionally misrepresent the facts to suit ideological interests (Apple, 2014)? While it may be tempting to oppose textbook (or other) reductions on these grounds, these concerns arise through an over-simplification of the opposition between the textbook representation and the 'real' or primary sources. The history of pedagogical representation illustrates well these issues.

It has been widely argued that one of the key conditions that gave rise to the Protestant Reformation and so the Catechism was the printing press (see Postman, 1995, chapter 2). This period of transformation also led, in 1658, to the publication of a key text in the history of pedagogical representation and reduction, often understood as the first textbook for children: John Comenius' *Orbis Sensualism Pictus* (*The Visible World in Pictures*). This text is important because it is arguably one of the last attempts to encompass and represent the whole cosmos (including things invisible) into a single pedagogical work: the 'textbook' form of pedagogical reduction, we might say. Subsequent efforts towards encyclopaedism had to confront the increasing challenges of a cosmos 'unmade' (Randles, 1999) – without the binding force and order of the great chain of being – and with the increasing knowledge brought into view by the new philosophers. As these complex changes unfolded, it has been argued that they created the conditions for the early constructions of childhood (Postman, 1995), constructions that themselves led to the need for the self-conscious pedagogical reduction of the world. It is at this point, argues Mollenhauer (2013), that we see children not just being present to an adult world, but that the world is self-consciously re-presented to children by way of pedagogical reductions. Furthermore, Mollenhauer refers to the associated idea that schools and classrooms became places for *pedagogical rehearsal*: educational places are not 'real world' since they are precisely set apart in order to offer students the opportunity to rehearse complex actions, knowledges, and attitudes before they are performed for 'real.' These processes of and spaces for representation, reduction and rehearsal are vital in positioning pedagogical reductions within the broader sweep of educational history.

So, we see that the idea of pedagogical reduction applies to secular teaching materials such as general textbooks and schemes of work, all of which are involved in making selections from fields of knowledge in order to give material form to subject domains. Educators make judgements about the kinds of interpretation of phenomena that most effectively support the students, and the sequence in which those representations are best presented, by providing select narratives, and examples.[6] Other principles are at play here, but I hope to have given a plausible account of the idea that interpretive representation is necessary, and that there are reasons to call this a process of reduction. Not only is this kind of reductive interpretation necessary, but it is a constructive and formative process: it is precisely through the aperture of the reduction that something can come into view at all. I now want to discuss similar issues with the idea of reduction particularly in the context of religion and RS/RE, issues that the example of the Catechism has already anticipated.

4   Reductionism and Religious Education

In the context of interpreting religion, reduction has a bad name. It is quite common for theories of religion to be negatively characterised as reductive: Karl Marx, Sigmund Freud, or James Frazer being cases in point. Here religion is framed as the epiphenomena of the real economic, psychological or historical forces at work. However, in debates of religion (and other issues), calling something you don't like "reductionist" seems like an inadequate strategy that has probably had its day, since any general process of scientific reasoning depends upon some elements of generalisation. Occam's razor, for instance, is properly reductive. As discussed in the previous section, it is not reduction in itself that is the problem, but rather how it is deployed and how complete the reduction is thought to be: to anticipate the discussion that follows, the concept of pedagogical reduction does not only concern the curriculum content, but also the process by which that curriculum is made present. In other words, it is not just about what, but also about *how* the world is reduced.

The desire of so-called phenomenologists of religion, like Max Scheler, Mircea Eliade, Rudolf Otto, and Ninian Smart, to allow the phenomena of religion to speak for themselves, or for some version of Clifford Geertz's thick description to be methodologically predominant does not ultimately let us off the reductive hook, since interpretation is not eliminated by thickening our descriptions and accounts, or by attempting to be purely descriptive. Without getting into a developed discussion of the relationship between phenomenology and hermeneutics, let me simply say that the view I am taking here is that there is no uninterpreted phenomena to which we can refer: as soon as reference is made, then also interpretation is made. (There might be uninterpreted phenomena to which we cannot refer, allowing it, then to remain uninterpreted, but reference to that would entail a paradox!).

I earlier suggested that reductionism sees the representation of phenomena as necessary and sufficient for complete understanding, while from the perspective of pedagogical reduction the representation of phenomena is necessary but never complete. When we turn to the pedagogical reduction of religion, we can see how these two tendencies bring about a particular tension. In this chapter I can only make some brief remarks about this so let me suggest that there are two general forces at work in the re-presentation of religion. On the one hand calls for greater religious literacy are underpinned by a desire to ensure that diverse religious traditions and communities are understood in all their complexity and richness (Dinham & Francis, 2015; Shaw, 2020). Here university professors of Religious Studies, like Jonathan Z. Smith are troubled by the reductive representations enacted through the world religions paradigm so common to RS and RE (Smith, 1978). On the other hand, 'understanding religion' entails some form of simplification, generalisation and representation. This dichotomy is played out in various ways, but the point of my argument is that a theory of pedagogical reduction would help us make more considered choices concerning the ways religions are interpreted and represented pedagogically.

The scholars of Religious Studies often emphasise the complexity of religious traditions, showing them not to be uniform and singular entities with clear cut boundaries and definitive distinguishing features. Definitions are provisional, arguments historically framed, and religions thereby must be understood as internally pluralistic, contested, with porous boundaries, and involving immanent critique. In other words, it has become orthodox to point out that there is no singular and discrete Christianity, Islam, Judaism and so on, rather there are multiple forms of any tradition each being historically, socially, geographically, and culturally formed and inflected. Not only is there pluralism within religious traditions, but that pluralism shows that the lines between orthodoxy and heterodoxy are themselves historically framed and constructed.

The recognition of this complexity presents systematic analysis of religion with various problems, most particularly, of course, the problem of determining the nature of the subject matter: what does and does not count as a *religion*. Do the beliefs and practices that fall under the general rubric of Hinduism constitute a 'religion' (Flood, 1996)? To what extent do the principles and practices of Confucianism define it as a religion (Fan, 2011)? How are forms of Christian atheism or humanist spirituality positioned among the general questions of understanding religion? Some of these discussions might be interpreted in terms of Tröhler's research knowledge rather than pedagogical knowledge, but these are academic questions which bear upon the ways in which religious ideas are presented pedagogically. Here we must admit that the distinction between academic and pedagogical knowledge is itself fluid. The desire to correct a simplistic view of Hinduism is both academic and pedagogical in the terms presented by Tröhler. That we might want to include Confucianism or forms of Humanism in theories of religion, reflect changing social and political priorities. It seems likely that these interpretations of Hinduism or Confucianism, for instance, are determined by political interests: for instance, it is hardly surprising that contemporary neo-Confucianism is quite clearly not associated with conventional religion in China's contemporary self-understanding, and that therefore Confucianism is reinterpreted aesthetically rather than religiously.

So, if I am to make a case for the pedagogical reduction of religion, I cannot imagine that conventional forms of RE, and the reductions they employ, are without prejudice. On the other hand, it should be clear that I am not making a case for leaving the prejudices of contemporary RE unexamined. On the contrary, the examination of those prejudices precisely depends upon a better articulated theory of pedagogical reduction so that the interests governing the pedagogical reduction are made explicit so that different, better informed interpretations might also be in view. If a good deal of the scholarship is undertaken by European and American scholars (even more particularly, white men within those contexts) then the pedagogical reductions are likely to reflect certain perceptions of, and assumptions about, the world. The ways in which Hindu religious traditions and practices, or indigenous forms of religious life in First Nations communities of North America, are framed by religious categories imported from broadly Christian intellectual traditions has been noted by scholars of religion (Lewin, 2016). So surely some historical consciousness on the part of the interpreters is desirable if we are to do better in terms of how inclusive we can be with our interpretive re-presentations of religion.

5   Pedagogical Reduction in the Representation of Religion

On the one hand we can be justifiably circumspect about generalising and presenting religious phenomena in reductive ways, while on the other hand, we must accept that pedagogy is intrinsically interpretive, and therefore reductive. Indeed, I have argued that this is not only an unfortunate necessity but is the very possibility of showing the world at all. I have noted that reduction is both a process (of reducing) and a product (the selected/simplified object). Thus, speaking educationally, reduction involves consideration of *how* to re-present the world, and *what* to select from the world. I believe we need to consider not only the extent to which the curriculum content fairly represents a given subject matter, we must also consider how that 'content' is made present in the practices of education. For this reason, the next step in my argument considers how we make judgements about the appropriateness of reduction of religion by introducing the concept of *pedagogical tact*, a kind of practical wisdom (*phronesis*). Pedagogical tact is a faculty that bears upon all aspects of education, including representation, and encourages practitioners to consider and reflect upon the relations between theoretical understanding of pedagogy, experience of educating, and reflection on experience (van Manen, 1992; Friesen & Osguthorpe, 2017).

Pedagogical tact describes the practical insight concerning how to use (among other things) pedagogical representations and reductions in ways that involve *give and take*. Because of the ambivalent nature of pedagogical reduction (that it both reveals and conceals) it is vital that educators pay attention to the students' relation to it in order to determine when to give and to take any particular pedagogical representation and reduction. The practical emphasis of pedagogical tact means there can be no universal rule for its application, and therefore no universal rules for how to reduce phenomena, or how to employ any particular pedagogical reduction, because educational representation involves the complex interaction between the conditions of learning set up by a teacher (which includes re-presenting phenomena) and the particular approach, experience and disposition of the student. The question of the accuracy of a representation is incomplete where it does not also take account of the disposition and capacity of the learner (i.e., *Bildsamkeit*: see Mollenhauer, 2013), something that educators do all the time, more or less reflectively, in their planning and practice. Representations can be understood as relational, and are, therefore, always enacted within the complex practices of education. The idea of a complete representation is not only theoretically implausible, but it fails to consider the practical relations between educator and student. The basic principle here is familiar to most teachers: that good teaching entails attention to all sorts of spatial, temporal and curricula conditions for growth, which also means employing the appropriate reduction at the right moment, taking account of all the contextual factors including the disposition(s) of the student(s).

But I want to take these observations about the proper place of reduction in RE one step further because although reduction is a general feature of education, it has particular implications if we consider the referent of RE. In other words, what are the pedagogical reductions of RE drawing attention to? What is the 'curriculum content' of RE? How do we represent that subject matter? It is not at all obvious what we are drawing attention to in RE, and any statement I make on this matter would elide the contested nature of the answer that I could give. In the context of the Catechism, attention is drawn to the gospel, but even this statement is ambiguous, for it is not clear whether the gospel here refers to the Biblical text, or Christ himself as the word of God. In other words, does the pedagogical reduction draw the student's attention to another representation, or to some other referent, something that exceeds representation (whatever that might mean)?

On the one hand, this is an issue of what RE is for: we might interpret RE simply in terms of the knowledge about various different religious traditions, where students are encouraged to understand the experiences, practices and beliefs of communities as social and cultural phenomena. In this respect, notwithstanding all the issues discussed thus far, RE shares the general problem of reduction with all other areas of the curriculum. Insofar as it is a general pedagogical issue, then one answer is to acknowledge that the quest for 'completeness' of experience or content is unhelpful when it comes to understanding religion (or anything else, for that matter), since it impossible to learn about all religious traditions in ways that are anything other than superficial. For this reason, Wagenschein warns against the temptation of completeness arguing that we must offer exemplary forms (Wagenschein, 2014). This might mean departing from, or deconstructing, the construction of the big 5 religions since sticking to the conventional approach might mean that students are not encouraged to go outside of their comfort zones or encouraged to look at margins. It may be that examination of the marginal forms of religious identity (e.g., Wicca or Jediism) will have far greater pedagogical resonance than any standard approach.

But often RE is said to seek something more: something like an existential encounter with something, or, as RE practitioners in England and Wales are aware, the concept of not only 'learning about,' but also 'learning from' religion (Engebretson, 2009). This seems to raise the intractable question of theological representation and mediation, itself the fulcrum on which the transformations of the Reformation turned. If we do wish to pursue this line in RE, then I would argue that the *theological* reference point for academic knowledge and pedagogical knowledge can only be referred to in complex, ambivalent, and ultimately insufficient ways, and so these forms of knowledge share a fundamental condition of insufficiency and uncertainty. Reference to the sufficient nature of the catechism must, then be interpreted pedagogically (or, more generally performatively), rather than literally. It is for this reason, that many religious traditions have attempted to subvert the terms which are used to mediate the theological reference point: by suggesting that what is posited by theology as god-talk, must also be undone by way of the *via negativa*.

This seems to rely on a notion of RE as being basically confessional which, no doubt, many would question. Yet, any straightforward distinction between confessional and non-confessional RE is itself a simplification (a reduction) that can't be generally applied. What it means to *understand* the phenomena of religion requires, I argue, a sense of the meaning of the religion which begins to erode the distinction between confessional and non-confessional RE. In brief, the secular 'neutral' framing of religions is by no means a perspective from nowhere: it enacts its own logic of what 'understanding' is (Lewin, 2016). Like any pedagogical reduction, this secular reduction can be given, but also must be taken, as part of the dialectics of religious understanding, a kind of *via negativa*.

6   Conclusion

In this chapter I have attempted to apply a general theory of pedagogical reduction to the field of RS/RE, a field in which concerns around explanatory reductionism lead to a general suspicion of pedagogical reduction more broadly. I have argued that although reflection on the criteria governing pedagogical reduction is essential for avoiding misrepresentation, we cannot avoid reduction itself: that pedagogical reduction must be distinguished from reductionism. My goal has been to consider the process of understanding the theories and practices, as well as the scope and limits of pedagogical reduction; that is, the art of forming, giving and taking those reductions appropriately in part through the practices of pedagogical tact. The point of pedagogical tact is not to offer general criteria for knowing what good application of tact looks like, since, by definition, tact involves the particular case, not the general rules. It is about developing an awareness of when and how to apply the general principles of (in this instance) pedagogical reduction. This raises further questions of how pedagogical tact can be reliably developed in educators, a question that I have no simple answer for, but which suggests a complex discussion of the relation between theory and practice (Lewis, 2018; Somr & Hrušková, 2014).

The art of giving and taking representations is something that religions, in general, have contemplated for a very long time, and they offer forms of discourse and practices of contemplation (such as the *via negativa*, or the aesthetics of religious life) that allow for more flexible notions of representation. For this reason, I argue that dialogue between religious and pedagogical histories would be fruitful in understanding, reflecting upon, and enacting pedagogical reductions.

Notes

1   For the sake of simplicity, I use Religious Education (RE) to refer to teaching of/about religion in schools and colleges, and Religious Studies (RS) to refer to teaching of/about religion in universities.
2   Critical questions around representation also exist in geography, history and other social or human sciences, but the so-called physical and mathematical sciences appear to be less obviously bound to particular social and historical narratives. This is complex, however, since it can be argued that any kind of representation entails the exercise of power.
3   Much of what follows builds upon the distinction between presentation and representation made by Mollenhauer (2013).
4   Gadamer calls it the miracle of understanding: "The task of hermeneutics is to clarify this miracle of understanding, which is not a mysterious communion of souls, but sharing in a common meaning" (Gadamer, 2002, p. 292).
5   Reference to the concept of reduction can be found here and there. For instance, Dewey writes that "[t]he inequality of achievement between the mature and the immature not only necessitates teaching the young, but the necessity of this teaching gives an immense stimulus to reducing experience to that order and form which will render it most easily communicable and hence most usable" (Dewey, 1916, p. 7).
6   Although the concept of the exemplary is also not widely discussed in educational theory, there is more work here: see, for instance, Dahlbeck and Korsgaard (2020). Wolfgang Klafki and Martin Wagenschein have developed influential *didaktik* analyses which focus on the exemplary (Klafki, 2015; Wagenschein, 2015).

References

An Ageless Summary of an Everlasting Comfort. (2019). http://www.heidelberg-catechism.com/en/

Apple, M. (2014). *Official knowledge*. Routledge.

Becker, A., & Jenny, S. (2017). No need for training wheels: Ideas for including balance bikes in elementary physical education. *Journal of Physical Education, Recreation & Dance, 88*(4), 14–21.

Bierma, L. (2005). *An introduction to the Heidelberg Catechism: Sources, history, and theology*. Baker Publishing Group.

Cotter, C., & Robertson, D. G. (Eds.). (2016). *After world religions: Reconstructing religious studies*. Routledge.

Dahlbeck, J., & Korsgaard, M. (2020). Introduction: The role of the exemplar in Arendt and Spinoza. Insights for moral exemplarism and moral education. *Ethics and Education, 15*(2), 135–143.

Dewey, J. (1916). *Democracy and education*. Macmillan.

Dinham, A., & Francis, M. (Eds.). (2015). *Religious literacy in policy and practice*. Policy Press.

Dreyer, W. (2014). The Heidelberg Catechism: A 16th century quest for unity. *HTS Teologiese Studies/Theological Studies, 70*(1), Art. 2092. http://dx.doi.org/10.4102/hts.v70i1.2092

Dreyfus, H. (1992). *What computers still can't do: A critique of artificial reason*. MIT Press.

Engebretson, K. (2009). Learning about and learning from religion. The pedagogical theory of Michael Grimmitt. In M. de Souza, G. Durka, K. Engebretson, R. Jackson, & A. McGrady (Eds.), *International handbook of the religious, moral and spiritual dimensions in educa*tion (pp. 667–678). Springer.

Fan, R. (Ed.). (2011). *The renaissance of Confucianism in contemporary China*. Springer.

Flood, G. (1996). *An introduction to Hinduism*. Cambridge University Press.

Flood, G. (2011). *The importance of religion: Meaning and action in our strange world*. Wiley-Blackwell.

Friesen, N., & Osguthorpe, R. (2017). Tact and the pedagogical triangle: The authenticity of teachers in relation. *Teaching and Teacher Education, 70*(1), 255–264.

Gadamer, H. G. (2002). *Truth and method*. Continuum.

Gallagher, S. (2006). Where's the action? Epiphenomenalism and the problem of free will. In S. Pocket, W. Banks, & S. Gallagher (Eds.), *Does consciousness cause behaviour?* (pp. 109–124). MIT Press.

Gallagher, S. (2018). Rethinking nature: Phenomenology and a non-reductionist cognitive science. *Australasian Philosophical Review, 2*(2), 125–137.

Harvey, G. (2013). *Food, sex and strangers: Understanding religion as everyday life*. Acumen.

Heidegger, M. (1977). *The question concerning technology and other essays*. Harper & Row.

Klafki, W. (2015). Didactic analysis as the core of preparation of instruction. In I. Westbury, S. Hopmann, & K. Riquarts (Eds.), *Teaching as a reflective practice: The German didaktik tradition* (pp. 85–107). Routledge.

Idinopulos, T., & Yonan, E. (Eds.). (1993). *Religion and reductionism: Essays on Eliade, Segal, and the challenge of the social sciences for the study of religion*. Brill.

Lewin, D. (2016). *Educational philosophy for a post-secular age*. Routledge.

Lewin, D. (2019). Toward a theory of pedagogical reduction: Selection, simplification and generalisation in an age of critical education. *Educational Theory, 68*(3), 495–512.

Lewin, D. (2020). Between horror and boredom: Fairy tales and moral education. *Ethics and Education, 15*(2), 213–231. doi:10.1080/17449642.2020.1731107

Lewis, T. (2018). Can one teach tact? *Philosophy of Education Yearbook Archive, 2018*(1), 310–314.

Masschelein, J., & Simons, M. (2013). *In defence of school: A public issue*. E-ducation, Culture & Society.

Masuzawa, T. (2005). *The invention of world religions, or, how European universalism was preserved in the language of pluralism*. University of Chicago Press.

Online Etymology Dictionary. (2019). https://www.etymonline.com/word/educe

Owen, S. (2011). The world religions paradigm: Time for a change. *Arts & Humanities in Higher Education, 10*(3), 253–268.

Postman, N. (1995). *The disappearance of childhood*. Vintage Books.

Randles, W. (1999). *The unmaking of the medieval Christian cosmos, 1500–1760: From solid heavens to boundless æther*. Routledge.

Rochmann, B. (2011). *Bye-Bye, training wheels. Hello, balance bike*. http://healthland.time.com/2011/09/30/bye-bye-training-wheels-hello-balance-bikes-learning-to-ride-a-bike-has-never-been-so-easy/

Segal, R. (1983). In defense of reductionism. *Journal of the American Academy of Religion, 51*(1), 97–124.

Shaw, M. (2020). Towards a religiously literate curriculum: Religion and worldview literacy as an educational model. *Journal of Beliefs & Values, 41*(2), 150–161. doi:10.1080/13617672.2019.1664876

Shepherd, N. (2014). *The living mountain*. The Canons.

Smart, N. (1996). *Dimensions of the sacred: Anatomy of the world's beliefs*. Harper Collins.

Smith, J. Z. (1978). *Map is not territory: Studies in the history of religions*. University of Chicago Press.

Somr, M., & Hrušková, L. (2014). Herbart's philosophy of pedagogy and educational teaching. *Studia Edukacyjne, 33*, 413–429.

Tröhler, D. (2008). The knowledge of science and the knowledge of the classroom: Using the Heidelberg Catechism (1563) to examine overlooked connections. In E. Campi, S. De Angelis, A. Goeing, & A. Grafton (Eds.), *Scholarly knowledge: Textbooks in early modern Europe* (pp. 75–86). Librarie Droz.

Van Manen, M. (1992). *The tact of teaching: Meaning of pedagogical thoughtfulness*. The Althouse Press.

Vlieghe, J., & Zamojski, P. (2019). *Towards an ontology of teaching: Thing-centred pedagogy, affirmation and love for the world*. Springer.

Wagenschein, M. (2015). Teaching to understand: On the concept of the exemplary in teaching. In I. Westbury, S. Hopmann, & K. Riquarts (Eds.), *Teaching as a reflective practice: The German didaktik tradition* (pp. 161–175). Routledge.

CHAPTER 5

'Buddhism Is Not a Religion, But Paganism Is': The Applicability of the Concept of 'Religion' to Dharmic and Nature-Based Traditions, and the Implications for Religious Education

Denise Cush and Catherine Robinson

Abstract

This chapter explores the concept of religion in popular, academic and adherent usage, and in particular whether it is at all helpful when applied to Dharmic or Nature-based traditions. Problems include the homogenisation of diversity and the construction of separate and unified systems of beliefs and practices which have affected portrayals of 'Eastern' traditions, including in religious education. It concludes by examining the importance for religious education of opening up the debate about what is meant by 'religion,' and of including the study of Dharmic traditions, a wider range of worldviews and new forms of 'being religious' from an early age.

Keywords

religion – Dharmic religions – religious education – Paganism

1 Introduction

The recent report of the Commission on Religious Education in England (CoRE, 2018) suggested changing the name of the subject previously known as 'Religious Education,' or at examination level for students aged 16+ and 18+, 'Religious Studies,' to 'Religion and Worldviews.' The rationale for this proposal was not only to include non-religious worldviews as part of the content of the subject, but, by putting 'religion' in the singular, both to clarify the main emphasis of the field of study, and also to draw attention to the need to problematise the concept of 'religion' and related concepts such as 'secularity,' 'spirituality' and 'worldview.' Religious education can no longer take place as if there are simple definitions and shared understanding of such terms. So important was this felt to be that this was listed as one of the nine items proposed as the 'National Entitlement to the Study of Religion and Worldviews' for all pupils in England (CoRE, 2018, p. 12).

2   Popular Understanding of 'Religion'

'Religion' is, like many other terms, used in everyday discourse with the presumption that there is a shared understanding between speaker/writer and audience/reader. However, it does not take long to realise that this is not necessarily the case, although there is usually sufficient overlap between understandings for the conversation to make some sort of sense. Scholars and journalists who examine how the word is understood in popular discourse point out that for many people today 'religion' has negative associations, to the extent that Linda Woodhead (2016b) called it a 'toxic brand.' For many, she found, 'religion' is associated with organisations discredited by scandals, holding illiberal social attitudes, and preaching unthinking obedience to authorities.

In recent decades, scholars have noted the sharp increase in the number of people identifying as 'not religious' in censuses and surveys in Europe and the USA. Woodhead (2016b) suggested that December 2015 was the tipping point where the 'nones' reached 50% in the UK, with higher percentages the younger the age group asked. Further research has revealed that those who tick 'none' on surveys are not necessarily atheist or humanist but may engage in private spiritual practice that others might label 'religious' or even believe in God (see Woodhead, 2016a). Simeon Wallis' research (2014) with secondary school pupils who claimed to be 'nones' revealed that what 'religion' implies to many young people who reject it tends to include propositional metaphysical beliefs that they do not share, 'strict' morality, and organisations that they would not wish to join. They tend to apply the label 'religious' only to those who accept the whole package of a particular religious worldview and are thoroughgoing in their practice. Often, 'religion' is not a topic they spend much time thinking about – their main concerns are elsewhere. Yet compared with previous generations, younger people tend to be tolerant of religious diversity, seeing this as a matter of personal choice, but in the words of journalist Andrew Brown (2016) "religion has become something that other people do." According to Linda Woodhead, among young people "recent research suggests a high level of interest in religion even though commitment to a particular religion may be low" (Woodhead, 2016b, p. 11). They can see the relevance of learning about 'other people's' religions (in RE lessons or elsewhere) whilst not wanting to 'be religious' themselves.

As fewer people (and even fewer young people) have direct personal experience of actively belonging to a religious community, their knowledge of 'religion,' apart from in RE lessons, increasingly comes second-hand via the 'media.' Religion as reported by the news media tends naturally to focus on the controversial and sensational, which tends to reinforce the negative image of 'religion.' John Holroyd claims that "the receipt of hard, quite often negative news about religion by a highly secularised public is, in the long view, a new phenomenon" (Holroyd, 2019, p. 37). He goes on to point out that even the more responsible channels which seek to present a 'balanced' view, tend to achieve that balance by choosing spokespeople of opposing polarised viewpoints. These are often not very representative of the run-of-the-mill majority in the tradition in question, who would not be as interesting to read about/ hear. The pressure to reduce everything to a quotable soundbite oversimplifies many a very nuanced issue. Thus whereas 'religion' is increasingly present and discussed in the public realm, the combination with a decrease in first hand practice and knowledge of religion has created a situation where, according to sociologists such as Davie and Dinham (see Dinham & Francis, 2015), there is a general lack of 'religious literacy' just when it is needed, leading to a poor quality of public debate.

3   Academic Discussion of 'Religion'

It is not surprising to find that there is much debate about the term 'religion' amongst those professionally involved with Religious Studies at University level. Most would agree with Wilfred Cantwell Smith (1978) that the term 'religion' as currently conceived is a construct both modern and western, especially the understanding of 'a religion' as a separate and identifiable unified system of beliefs.

In a book first published in 1962, Smith charts the changes in the Western use of the term 'religion,' noting that it was only in the modern period marked by the Renaissance, Reformation, Enlightenment and later developments that the concept acquired great significance. Not only is it a Western term with no real equivalents in other traditions but it turns 'religion' into a static entity, a thing, an objectification he dubs 'reification.' Vivienne Baumfield, in her recent appreciation of Smith's influential publication, explains this as "a process of misplaced concreteness" which leads to "essentialist definitions which obscure the dialectical relationship between personal faith and its collective worldly expression in a cumulative tradition" (Baumfield, 2019, p. 115). Whether one follows Smith in preferring the terms 'faith' for the individual, personal experience and 'tradition' for the ongoing collective to the word 'religion,' it is important to see that this is not just another tedious academic debate about the exact meaning of words, but has dangerous practical consequences. When this reified term is then used to construct a series of separate monolithic 'isms,' religions plural, they are seen as static entities, in separate silos from each other and from the secular or everyday world, and as competitors set against each other, 'us' and 'them.' This understanding of 'religion' can serve to cause people to make sweeping generalisations about, for example, 'all Muslims,' and in the worst-case scenario be a contributing factor to hate crimes or war. Both 'faith' and 'tradition' have become much-used alternatives for the word 'religion' whether the debt to Smith is recognised or not.

So, one problem with the term 'religion' is that it became a separate category during the 18th century Enlightenment, distinguished from both philosophy and everyday life, and reified into a 'thing.' A further problem is that the category was modelled on the tradition best known in Europe, Christianity, especially Protestant Christianity. This led to scholars encountering other traditions elsewhere in the world to look for parallels to elements such as God, scripture, doctrine, faith, church and thus distort the complex realities they were exploring.

It is also pointed out by scholars such as Richard King (1999) that the idea of Religious Studies as an academic discipline, distinct from Theology in being an objective, secular and scientific study, also arose from the thinking of the European Enlightenment, and that the study of religion and the concept of religion were a process of mutual creation, comparable to the 'iatrogenic' effect of illnesses caused by the treatment or suggestions of a doctor, the supposed subject matter being created by the processes of scholarship.

Timothy Fitzgerald (1995, 2000) argues that the very existence of 'Religious Studies' that studies something called 'religion' is actually covert theology, in that it presumes there is an essence to the concept of religion, and thus that there is a transcendent something to study. It is perhaps relevant to note that many of the pioneers of Religious Studies/Study of Religions as a discipline in universities and also non-confessional, multifaith religious education in schools were not secularists but liberal Christians. Fitzgerald suggests ditching the concept of 'religion' and seeing it as an aspect of 'culture,' to be studied as part of 'Cultural Studies.' However, this suggestion has not had much appeal, as similar issues emerge when trying to define 'culture,' and exploring 'religion' through the lens of Cultural Studies might detract from full coverage of what the term currently delineates, not to mention alienating many of the adherents of what is being studied.

Both Smith and Fitzgerald would do away with the term 'religion,' but we still need a word to refer to the area of human experience we are trying to discuss, and alternatives such as 'faith,' 'tradition' or 'culture' are also problematic ('faith' is perhaps too protestant Christian, 'tradition' with too little space for individual experience, 'culture' too associated with the arts and with a built-in presumption that everything is made up by humans ...).

Jonathan Z. Smith suggests a 'middle way.' We should accept that 'religion' is a scholarly concept that can be defined as required and serves to describe the focus of the subject (Smith, 1998, pp. 281–282). It is his view that a distinction should be drawn between religion as a concept and those beliefs and practices deemed religious, denying that there is any object in reality to which religion refers but insisting that religion is a heuristic device useful for purposes of analysis and classification (Smith, 1982, p. xi). So, we can both accept that there is no such object as 'religion' out there in reality, and continue to use the term, but always conscious that it is merely a conceptual tool that needs constant critique.

Russell T. McCutcheon asserts that it is actually "the malleability of this term, religion, that today strikes some scholars as so interesting" (McCutcheon, 2017a, p. 5), and in his evaluation of the future currency of the term, argues that we should be particularly aware of its recent use in legal and political contexts, asking "might calling something religious be itself a political act ... a tactical way of managing people?" (McCutcheon, 2017b, p. 302). He concludes that it is up to each of us to be aware of and critique how the term is used by ourselves and others. "It is therefore [*the reader's*] term, to be defined as *they* see fit, in contrast to how others may define and use it – all of whom are trying to affect the world in who knows what ways." (McCutcheon, 2017a, p. 305). This somewhat contrasts with J. Z. Smith's view of this as a scholarly project.

In the light of this suggestion of deciding upon and clarifying one's own understanding of 'religion,' here are a few the current authors and others have found interesting. There are those that stress the ongoing collective developments, such as Danielle Hervieu-Léger's (2000) 'chain of memory,' emphasising the idea of an authoritative tradition passed down from one's ancestors, or James Cox's 'identifiable communities' with 'postulated alternative realities' (Cox, 2009, pp. 101–103). On the other hand, there are those which stress more the individual and existential such as Phillip Goodchild's 'response to the most significant limits of experience' (Goodchild, 2004, p. 168). Any definition needs to reflect the fact that the area of human experience that the term seeks to delineate is about emotions, values, customs and practices both ritual and ethical, and identity as well as beliefs, and, usually, about what people consider of most importance in their lives.

4 Adherents' Views on the Term 'Religion'

It might be more surprising to find that some adherents of religious traditions also have problems with the term 'religion' to describe their worldviews. Examples would include many Jehovah's Witnesses who reject the term for describing their own faith while reserving it for other faith groups which are seen as human inventions. For similar reasons, Dietrich Bonhoeffer called for a 'religionless Christianity,' where 'religion' is viewed as a human creation which can impede the authentic relationship with God. There are adherents of just about every religious worldview who can be heard (or read) arguing that their tradition 'is not a religion but a way of life.' A quick internet search of 'not a religion, a way of life' in 2017 revealed examples from Islam, Buddhism, Christianity, Hinduism and Native American traditions.

It is tempting to conclude that if the general public, many religious studies scholars and adherents of a wide range of religions reject the term 'religion,' can we really continue to use it? Certainly not without many caveats, qualifications and discussion.

5 Dharmic Traditions

As the term 'religion' and dominant understandings of its meaning has been shown to be a 'western' development, it is not surprising to find that it does not fit very well with 'eastern' traditions. In addition to the problems of reification and essentialism, the application of a western term to eastern traditions has distorted understanding further. Western scholars of eastern traditions were often undertaking their work in a context of colonialism and imperialism, and thus the processes of categorisation had political motivations for managing the colonised. Edward Said coined the term 'Orientalism' to describe the way in which the East is defined by the West for its own purposes and in its own interests (see Said, 1995, p. 3). Identifying a religion in a particular way could be used to justify colonialism.

One feature of the Western understanding of religion is that each religion has clear boundaries, dividing it from other religions, and excluding the possibility of multiple allegiance. Paul Dundas comments on the dubious applicability of this notion to Indian religions when stressing that the various '-isms' may fail to capture the reality they purport to represent where religious observance has tended to be more fluid and dynamic in character (see Dundas, 2002, pp. 6–7). This directs attention to the often unexamined and unacknowledged ethnocentric assumptions that demarcate religion, including the separation into distinct exclusive traditions. Having separated out these traditions, there is also a tendency to see each 'ism' as a unitary entity, where all adherents are presumed to share the same beliefs and practices (see King, 2008, p. 578). Another Western assumption, on the model of post-Enlightenment understandings of Christianity, is that religion is predominantly about exclusive truth claims, whereas indigenous understandings may give priority to ritual practice (see Staal, 1989, p. 393).

Given the extent of distortion involved in constructing Asian traditions as religions in a Western sense, Fritz Staal goes so far as to claim that the imposition of the Western concept of religion on Asian traditions has led to the *invention* of Asian religions, so that Hindu-ism, Buddh-ism etc are false constructs of Western thought (see Staal, 1989, p. 393). Richard King modifies this by pointing out that indigenous people themselves were not just 'passive recipients' of other people's labels, but were themselves involved in the construction of 'religions' for their own purposes, so that it might be better to say that Eastern 'religions' are products of the colonial encounter (see King, 2008, p. 578). The following sections look in more detail at some of the 'Dharmic religions,' especially those that currently tend to be included in RE.

6   'Hindu-ism'

What is now called Hinduism is probably the most extreme case of the homogenisation of diversity. Kim Knott suggests that "there do seem to be many hinduisms rather than one Hinduism" (Knott, 1998, p. 114). Von Stietencron (cited in Oddie, 2008, p. 325) suggests that Vaishnavism, Shaivism and Shaktism can be seen as religions in their own right, comparable to the relationship between Judaism, Christianity and Islam. Scholars debate whether the idea of a single 'Hinduism' is a nineteenth-century creation or has much older roots – such as the encounter with Islam (see Oddie, 2008), but most agree that the concept of a unitary Hinduism was useful to both British colonial rulers and Hindu elites.

Today there are various influences involved in creating dominant constructions of Hinduism. One is the use of *sanatana dharma* as an indigenous equivalent to Hinduism, as Wilhelm Halbfass indicates, denoting the 'eternal religion' in a manner bearing the impress of a Christian or Western understanding of religion (see Halbfass, 1988, p. 344). The term was used in nineteenth century India to distinguish those who saw themselves as following traditional practice from the various reform movements (see Zavos, 2008, p. 756). It is often used today to describe Hindu temples in diaspora if they are not allied to any particular Hindu sect. It also fits well with some Western ideas of the unity of religions while also suggesting the superiority of Hinduism to more parochial exclusivist traditions.

Romila Thapar points out that the notion of 'Hinduism' in contemporary times has both favoured the elite Brahmanical tradition and high caste norms but also looked to Christianity (and Islam) for its pattern (see Thapar, 1985, p. 21). Teachers taking students on visits to Hindu temples in Western countries may have encountered this recasting of Hinduism in an Abrahamic mould by spokespersons seeking to make connections with the presumed Christian background of the visitors, by for example explaining that all the deities on view are different aspects of the one God, or that the *Bhagavad-Gita* is like the Bible. Thus the account of Hinduism may stress a monotheistic understanding of divinity either centred on *Brahman* as the essential unity of the selves in Self or on *deva* as personal deity, a focus on scripture be it the *Upanishads* or the *Bhagavad-Gita*, and a prophet (or the nearest equivalent) in Krishna as the counsellor of Arjuna (see Thapar, 1985, p. 18). This version of Hinduism is often reflected in RE text books, which are keen on including the *trimurti* of Brahma, Vishnu and Shiva as a parallel with the Christian Trinity, whereas it could be argued that other groupings of deities, such as the five which are the focus of *pancayata puja* (Ganesh, Surya, Vishnu, Shiva and the Goddess Devi) are more significant.

Another factor shaping the image of Hinduism that has implications for RE is the dominance of *Advaita Vedanta* both in the classical form associated with Shankara and in the revised form of neo-Vedanta pioneered by Swami Vivekananda and championed by the philosopher Sarvepalli Radhakrishnan among others. The former, albeit read in the light of the latter as Ninian Smart makes clear, has led to a tendency to marginalise or omit other schools of thought (see Smart, 1999, pp. 317–319). Thus, Hinduism is presented as a non-dual philosophy with an impersonal concept of the divine which is the only reality, and the personal deity or deities are viewed as less accurate, more metaphorical ways of expressing the same truth. The latter has informed and underwritten accounts of Hindu tolerance and the truth of all religions to which Eric Sharpe has drawn attention (see Sharpe, 1977, pp. 65–67). While Vivekananda interpreted Hinduism in Vedantic terms, emphasising that Hinduism recognised the unity of religion deriving from a common divine source thereby delegitimising discrimination and exclusivity (see Vivekananda, 1994,

p. 18), Radhakrishnan's commentary on the *Bhagavad-Gita* presented a positive image for the diversity of the tradition, many paths up the same mountain, that can then be extended to interreligious relations as a kind of Hindu universalism (see Radhakrishnan, 1957, p. 102).

A somewhat contrary tendency is the influence of new movements within the Hindu tradition that are open to Western adherents, notably the International Society for Krishna Consciousness (ISKCON), who have been very influential in educational contexts. ISKCON derives from the *bhakti* (devotional) tradition in Hinduism, and the *Dvaita* or dualistic strand of Hindu philosophy, where God is personal (Krishna) and the devotee seeks a relationship with rather than identity with the divine. Despite an earlier emphasis upon the distinctiveness of ISKCON, differentiated from 'Hinduism' by, for example, its monotheism and castelessness, a number of scholars have pointed to the 'Hinduisation' of ISKCON evident in the influx of devotees of Indian descent and consistent with the decision to reposition ISKCON as a form of Hinduism with which the preferred term *sanatana dharma* is equated (see King, 2007, p. 165; Nye, 2001, pp. 30–31; Rochford, 2013, pp. 23–25). Alongside this process, the 'Iskconisation' of Hinduism has also been identified by various scholars, reflecting the prominent part played by ISKCON in ministry to the Hindu community, marked by founding membership of Hindu umbrella organisations as well as the leadership role exercised in various fora including RE where ISKCON Educational Services makes a significant contribution (see Nye, 2001, pp. 133–134; Rochford, 2013, p. 28; Warrier, 2012, pp. 464–465).

Hindu nationalism has also shaped the image of Hinduism and thereby how it is portrayed in RE. While Hindu nationalism is by no means always primarily religious in character – for Vinayak Damodar Savarkar, for example, *Hindutva* was a broader cultural, ethnic and geographical category – it does take religious form notably in the Vishwa Hindu Parishad (World Hindu Council) that proposes a homogenised and codified version of Hinduism, and seeks to mobilise religious symbols and sentiments for political purposes as in the Ayodhya campaign for the ostensible liberation of Rama's birthplace (see Jaffrelot, 1996, pp. 26–27, 200–201, 402–403).

In the diaspora, this particular portrayal of Hinduism has had direct consequences for education. In the UK the publication of a textbook produced by the Vishwa Hindu Parishad (VHP) entitled *Explaining Hindu Dharma: A Guide for Teachers* (Prinya, 1996) attracted negative comment in the RE journal *Resource* (Mukti, 1997), in turn producing a strong defensive reaction (Prinya et al., 1998). What was at stake was the perceived political agenda of the textbook as well as other allegations concerning an overly positive and unproblematised portrayal of Hinduism (see Sharma, 2000). A similar controversy over the depiction of Hinduism in California's school textbooks arose in the USA (see Kurien, 2006, pp. 734–735). Such examples are a clear warning about the agenda of materials used, and the agenda of organisations with an interest, in Religious Education.

In conclusion, 'Hinduism' is as problematic a term as 'religion,' with its existence in reality and usefulness as a term disputed, and current understandings influenced by a range of factors and agenda.

7 'Buddh-ism'

Buddhism is also characterised by great diversity. "Buddhism in Sri Lanka, Buddhism in Tibet and Buddhism in Japan are as different on the surface as Christianity, Judaism and Islam" (Claxton, 1989, p. 6), so that the perception of a single unified system is also claimed to be a recent construct of Western scholars and Buddhist modernisers. As with other Dharmic traditions, in practice it is not so exclusive as this perception of Buddhism as a separate religion would imply – throughout the Buddhist world from Sri Lanka to Japan, 'Hindu' and other local deities are found in temples and sacred texts, as well as customs and practices.

In arguing for Buddhism as a distinct tradition, it might be argued that at it had a 'founder,' Siddhartha Gautama, the Buddha, who was conscious of forming a new community separate from the various other religious tendencies of his time. However, classifying the Buddha as a 'founder' is misleading as the intrareligious understanding is that the Dharma (truth/teaching) is eternal, and there are been many other Buddhas both past and future, and for Mahayana Buddhists, in the present.

Among the important influences on contemporary perceptions of Buddhism are tendencies described as 'Protestant Buddhism' and 'Buddhist Modernism,' which reflect both Western influence and the agency of indigenous scholars. 'Protestant Buddhism' originally proposed by Gananath Obeyesekere in relation to Theravada Buddhism in Sri Lanka, highlights the selective and critical appropriation of aspects of Protestant Christianity both in order to urge reform of the Buddhist tradition as it had developed and to resist Protestant Christian proselytisation (see Gombrich & Obeyesekere, 1988, pp. 215–224). The debt to Protestant Christianity is clear – the focus upon the laity, the rejection of ritual, the appeal to a scriptural model for reform of a contemporary Buddhism deemed to be corrupt and superstitious – but limited by the reinterpretation of the lay lifestyle in monastic terms, the performance of many rituals and, more generally, the maintenance of distinctive Buddhist doctrines (see Berkwitz, 2012, pp. 33–35; McMahan, 2012, pp. 162–163). Protestant Buddhism allows Buddhism to be classed as "a world religion … with its own founder, sacred scriptures and fixed body of doctrine" (Lopez, 2002, p. xiii) – in the same category as Christianity, only better, because more rational and scientific.

This portrayal of Buddhism as rational and scientific has been labelled 'Buddhist Modernism' (McMahan, 2008) or 'Modern Buddhism' (Lopez, 2002). This highlights the positive response to features of modernist discourse deriving from the European Enlightenment including rationalism and empiricism hence representing Buddhism as scientific by setting aside aspects of the traditional worldview while espousing a this-worldly ethic (see Bechert, 1973, p. 91; Lopez, 2002, pp. xi–xii). This representation not only portrays Buddhism in a manner intended to demonstrate its scientific credentials where science is privileged as a source of authority and a standard of judgement but also facilitates the establishment of a clear contrast with Christianity which becomes stereotyped as unscientific on the grounds, for example, of its belief in a creator deity and its issues with the theory of evolution (see McMahan, 2008, pp. 89–91). A good example of this presentation of a rational Buddhism, not based on faith or God, downplaying the ritual elements of popular Buddhism, and aimed at a Western audience, is the well-known book *What the Buddha Taught* by Walpola Rahula, first published in 1959, that in various ways embodies the characteristics of this modernist discourse though, as the title indicates, glossing any difference between the ancient teaching and its modern interpretation (see Rahula, 1990, pp. 1–8).

There is also a growing tendency, by both Buddhists and outsiders to claim that Buddhism is not a religion but a philosophy. This was noted by Gombrich and Obeyesekere (1988, pp. 221–222) as a feature of the Buddhist modernist discourse, on the grounds of its disavowal of deity and recourse to reason. The label 'religion' is often rejected for Buddhism where religion is defined as centring on faith or the God of monotheism. A recent example of preferring to use the term philosophy is found in a television programme presented by historian Bettany Hughes (2015), where she refers to the Buddha as 'the philosopher.' This tendency is also very likely to reflect the current negative image of the word 'religion' (see above) and more positive associations with the word 'philosophy.' There is evidence that the reputation of Buddhism as 'philosophical' has made it more popular with male students (see Fearn & Francis, 2004).

Stephen Batchelor advocates what he calls 'Secular Buddhism,' arguing for the need to replace the perception of Buddhism as religious belief centred on the concept of truth by an understanding of Buddhism as practice concerned with the alleviation of suffering (Batchelor, 2012, pp. 90–94). One of the examination providers for Religious Studies at A level (for students at 18+) draws teachers' attention to Stephen Batchelor's presentation of Buddhism as a secular philosophy, but also advises that students 'should consider the extent to which Batchelor's view of Buddhism is a distortion to suit a Western world view' (see Eduqas, 2016, p. 68) and that they should note the alternative view of Buddhism as a religion put forward by David Brazier (2014).

It is perhaps worth noting that Brazier represents (indeed leads) a Mahayana group. The emphasis on rationality tends to be more characteristic of Theravada modernisers. Western distortions of Mahayana Buddhism tend to be more of a romantic sort than rational kind, particularly when it comes to Tibetan traditions. Before leaving Buddhism, it might be worth noting that the understanding of labels as constructs rather than reality is an important part of Buddhist thinking. The term 'religion,' like 'self' may be viewed as "this denomination ... this designation, this conceptual term, a current appellation and a mere name" (*Questions of King Milinda* Conze, 1959, p. 149).

8   'Sikh-ism'

Sikhism is usually classed as a Dharmic tradition, as originating in an Indian context, and as using the Indian word *Dharma* in self-descriptions, but there are also similarities with the Abrahamic traditions, especially Islam, so this categorisation can be disputed. The Sikh tradition underwent significant change in the modern era that witnessed the creation of the '-isms,' understood as reified, bounded and exclusive religions. Historically, as Harjot Oberoi observes, this means that the distinctions now drawn between Sikh, Hindu and Muslim affiliations are anachronistic in respect of earlier eras and likewise the neo-orthodox Khalsa-centred definition of Sikh identity advocated by Tat Khalsa reformers given the existence of diverse Sikh movements and various forms of Sikh belief and practice (Oberoi, 1994, pp. 420–421). Even so, plurality has not been eliminated.

Following Roger Ballard, if the 'dharmic' or ethical and 'qaumic' or communal dimensions of Punjabi religion have recently acquired ascendancy in official fora, in the Sikh case the drive to return to what has been seen as pure teaching and assert the unity of Sikhs as a separate religiously-constituted community, this has not led to the 'panthic' or mystical or 'kismetic' or magical dimensions losing their hold, however much religious authorities including Sikh leaders have been suspicious of devotion to other masters and popular so-called superstitions (see Ballard, 1996). Thus Sikhism as conventionally defined illustrates broader problems in the construction of discrete religions based upon a partial and selective reading of each tradition, reflected in the 'World Religions approach' (or 'World Religions Paradigm') in Religious Education (also Religious Studies) that has been criticised by Ron Geaves as applying a Christian model to the study of other traditions (see Geaves, 1996). It also illustrates the different criteria, implicitly or even explicitly, informing what is believed to constitute a 'World Religion' since Britain's imperial history and the presence of a substantial Sikh community has led to Sikhism being included in the RE curriculum in England, Wales and Scotland and more generally acquiring a prominent position where elsewhere it is often excluded, or marginalised.

9   Chinese 'Religions'

In an officially atheist state, which also claims to support freedom of religion, while complex legislation restricts religious practice in various ways (see Nai et al., 2020; Ye & Law, 2019; Zhou, 2018) religion is a topic of increasing interest, and to some extent increasing practice. Attitudes of young people, in such a different context, tend nevertheless to share some characteristics reminiscent of findings in England and other European countries. There is interest without necessarily wanting to join in, and a certain perception that while minority ethnic groups have religions (Muslim, Buddhist) the Han majority do not (see Ye & Law, 2019, p. 332). Although there is no subject equivalent to English RE, religions are sometimes included within other subjects such as history, geography or social studies in schools, but, depending on the textbook used, are likely to present religions as something of historical interest, as features of a pre-modern unscientific age, or as aspects of culture. This latter emphasis may have some positive things to say about the influence of religions, from an overall perspective of secular ethics.

An interesting question in the light of the definition of religion is whether Confucianism is a religion. It is not considered such in mainland China (where the list of religions is Buddhism, Daoism, Islam, Catholicism and Protestantism) or Taiwan (where the list of religions also includes Shinto, Mormonism, Unificationism ['Moonies'], and Kwan Tao.) Among Western scholars, there are very different views about the status of Confucianism as religious or even a religion, ranging from outright rejection to unequivocal acceptance. It may be classed rather as philosophy, or as an implicit background culture in both China and Japan. Or it may be viewed as religious, but in a different sense of the word. Part of the problem is the definition of religion in the light of the dominance of the Western model of religion shaped by the hegemony of Christianity. It is possible, as Roger Ames advocates, to disaggregate theism from religion, hence representing Confucianism as a non-theistic religion focused on human flourishing (see Ames, 2008, p. 479). Another related issue is the implications of the ethical and humanistic character of Confucian teaching. One argument advanced by Rodney Taylor appeals to the existence of an Absolute combined with a transformative individual relationship to it as demarcating religion, identifying the Absolute in Confucianism as *T'ien* and the sage as the ideal individual (see Taylor, 1998, pp. 84, 90).

10   Japanese 'Religions'

Many contemporary Japanese people claim to be 'non-religious' while simultaneously engaging in activities that others would call religious (see Reader, 1991, pp. 1–21). Buddhist temples and Shinto shrines are everywhere, people visit and engage in rituals and festivals. Hindu deities came to Japan as part of Buddhism, and feature in practice. However, all this activity is not considered to be 'religion,' as rather like with the young 'nones' in Britain, this term is associated with unwelcome Christian evangelising, organisations, belief systems, and dangerous 'cults.' There was not an indigenous term equivalent to 'religion' in the Western sense until the 19th century when *Shukyo* ('sect-teaching') was coined as a translation. Again, Japanese practice is non-exclusive, the same people may visit both Shinto shrines and Buddhist temples, welcome new babies in a Shinto ceremony and have a Buddhist funeral.

Brian Bocking points out that "like 'Hinduism,' Shinto is a portmanteau term for widely varying types and aspects of religion" (Bocking, 1996, p. viii). Although Shinto is often viewed as the indigenous religion of Japan, many scholars point out that the construction of 'Shinto' as the national religion, separated out from Buddhism, was a deliberate creation of the nineteenth century Meiji government (see Bocking, 1996, pp. viii–x). Bocking also points out that "the term Shinto has taken on a rather misleading aura of solidity and concreteness in Western writings that it has not enjoyed in Japan" (Bocking, 1996, pp. 173–174). Buddhism in Japan is diverse, including forms with origins in Japan and more recent Buddhist movements, and has had a complex relationship, including mutual influence and antagonism, with what has become known as Shinto. In addition, the Chinese traditions of Daoism and Confucianism have influenced Japanese thinking and practices, though not as 'separate and defined' religious entities (see Reader, 1998, p. 29).

Neither Chinese nor Japanese religions (other than Buddhism) are featured much in British RE, which has focused since the mid-1980s on six religions – Christianity, plus Buddhism, Hinduism, Islam, Judaism and Sikhism. Among the reasons for this are historical connections such as the British Empire and the size and visibility of contemporary communities in the UK. Elsewhere in the world Sikhism rarely features in RE and Chinese and Japanese religions may well be included. This serves to illustrate the parochial nature of any decision about what counts as a 'world religion,' another constructed category that has been much criticised (see for example Geaves, 1998).

11   The Case of Contemporary Pagan-ism and 'New Paradigm Religiosity'

Another group of traditions that do not fit very well with a concept of religion modelled on post-Enlightenment and Christian categories are those considered under the umbrella of 'contemporary Paganism.' This refers to the mostly polytheistic, pantheistic, or animist groups generally united by the focus on nature as sacred (for an overview see Cush, 2016). In the UK, this includes Druids, Wiccans, followers of Goddess Spirituality, and to some extent, Heathens. In contrast with traditions and individuals that want to dissociate themselves from 'religion,' Pagans have had to campaign to be accepted as a religion, with some successes only in the last decade. The Druid Network was accepted as a registered charity in 2010, and the Pagan Federation joined the Religious Education Council of England and Wales in 2011. Both the Pagan Federation and the Druid Network were accepted as members of the Interfaith Network in 2015.

In spite of claims to being the fastest growing religion, those who identify as Pagans are relatively small in number, though Pagan ideas and motifs have a wider influence. However, contemporary Paganism serves to illustrate what could be called a 'new paradigm religiosity.' In contrast to the stereotype of 'religion' discussed above, there is a stress on the individual, and individual experience as the source of authority. Ritual and ceremonies, stories and myths are more important than doctrines or dogmas. Ethical behaviour is not laid down in a series of commandments, but largely up to the individual and characterised by freedom, captured by the Wiccan 'rede': "an it harm none, do what thou wilt." Paganism tends to be eclectic, drawing upon several traditions, including Dharmic traditions ('karma') and Native American, Australian or other 'indigenous' spiritualities. Though there are Pagan organisations that can be joined, communication tends to be more through networking. The divine is immanent in nature (and in Nature) rather than transcendent. A further interesting feature is the conscious human creation of 'religion' – not only are Pagan ceremonies often scripted for the occasion by the participants, but even new deities (or at least new names) such as the goddess Nolava in Glastonbury are created.

12   Conclusion: Implications for Religious Education

As the term religion, though contested, is still very much in use, it would seem important to share with pupils from an early age the discussion of what people mean when they use words like religion/religious/not religious, and with older students discuss the constructed and contested nature of such concepts and reasons why people employ different definitions for different purposes in different contexts. Hence it was not conservatism or the influence of religious groups that led the Commission on RE to suggest that the new name for RE should be 'Religion and Worldviews,' rather than just 'Worldviews.'

The inclusion of Dharmic traditions, new forms of religiosity, as well as non-religious worldviews in the content of the subject from primary age would help to avoid creating a limited and reified concept of religion based solely on the Enlightenment/Christian model, and the fixing of associated views such as that religions are primarily about propositional truth claims, are unitary systems, are mutually exclusive, are necessarily about God, are either true or false, or find their main source of authority in texts.

The above suggestions would also help challenge the idea that an easy distinction can be made between the 'religious' and the 'non-religious' or 'secular,' in both theory and everyday practice, and avoid the impression given to the increasing number of pupils who do not identify as 'religious,' that religious education is about the study (whether found interesting or not) of other people's beliefs and customs rather than of relevance to their own developing worldviews.

References

Ames, R. T. (2008). *Li* and the a-theistic religiousness of classical Confucianism. In A. Eshleman (Ed.), *Readings in philosophy of religion: East meets west* (pp. 479–488). Blackwell Publishing.

Ballard, R. (1996). Panth, Kismet, Dharma te Qaum: Continuity and change in four dimensions of Punjabi religion. In P. Singh & S. S. Thandi (Eds.), *Globalisation and the region: Explorations in Punjabi identity* (pp. 7–38). Association for Punjab Studies.

Batchelor, S. (2012). A secular Buddhism. *Journal of Global Buddhism, 13,* 87–107.

Baumfield, V. (2019). Review of "the meaning and end of religion" by William Cantwell Smith. *British Journal of Religious Education, 41*(1), 115–116.

Bechert, H. (1973). Sangha, state, society, 'nation.' Persistence of traditions in 'post-traditional' Buddhist societies. *Daedalus, 102*(1), 85–95.

Berkwitz, S. C. (2012). Buddhism in modern Sri Lanka. In D. L. McMahan (Ed.), *Buddhism in the modern world* (pp. 29–47). Routledge.

Bocking, B. (1996). *A popular dictionary of Shinto.* Curzon.

Brazier, D. (2014). *Buddhism is a religion: You can believe it.* Woodsmoke Press.

Brown, A. (2016, January 20). No religion is the new religion. *The Guardian.* www.theguardian.com/commentisfree/2016/jan/20/no-religion-britons-atheism-christianity

Conze, E. (1959). *Buddhist scriptures.* Penguin.

CoRE (Commision on Religious Education). (2018). *Religion and worldviews: The way forward. A national plan for RE.* Final report. Religious Education Council of England and Wales. Retrieved April 3, 2020, from https://www.religiouseducationcouncil.org.uk/wp-content/uploads/2017/05/Final-Report-of-the-Commission-on-RE.pdf

Cox, J. L. (2009). Towards a socio-cultural, non-theological definition of religion. In D. L. Bird & S. J. Smith (Eds.), *Theology and religious Studies in higher education: Global Perspectives* (pp. 99–116). Continuum.

Claxton, G. (1989). *Buddhist lives.* Oliver & Boyd.

Cush, D., & Robinson, C. (2014). Developments in religious studies: Towards a dialogue with religious education. *British Journal of Religious Education, 36*(1), 4–17.

Cush, D., Robinson, C., & York, M. (Eds.). *The Routledge encyclopedia of Hinduism.* Routledge.

Cush, D. with Stygal, M. (2016). Paganism. *RE:ONLINE.* https://www.reonline.org.uk/subject-knowledge/paganism/

Dinham, A., & Francis, M. (Eds.). (2015). *Religious literacy in policy and practice.* Policy Press.

Dundas, P. (2002). *The Jains* (2nd ed.). Routledge.

Eduqas. (2016). *GCE A level in religious studies: Guidance for teaching.* https://www.eduqas.co.uk/qualifications/religious-studies/as-a-level/eduqas-a-level-religious-studies-gft-from-2016-e.pdf?language_id=1

Fearn, M., & Francis, L. (2004). From A-level to higher education: Student perceptions of teaching and learning in theology and religious studies. *Discourse, 3*(2), 58–91.

Fitzgerald, T. (1995). Religious studies as cultural studies: A philosophical and anthropological critique of the concept of religion. *DISKUS, 3*(1), 35–47.

Fitzgerald, T. (2000). *The ideology of religious studies.* Oxford University Press.

Geaves, R. (1996). Baba Balaknath: An exploration of religious identity. *DISKUS, 4*(2). http://jbasr.com/basr/diskus/diskus1-6/GEAVES.txt

Geaves, R. (1998). The borders between religions: A challenge to the world religions approach to religious education. *British Journal of Religious Education, 21*(1), 20–31.

Gombrich, R., & Obeyesekere, G. (1988). *Buddhism transformed: Religious change in Sri Lanka.* Princeton University Press.

Goodchild, P. (2004). Religious studies: What's the point (Conference). *Discourse, 3*(2), 161–172.

Halbfass, W. (1988). *India and Europe: An essay in understanding*. State University of New York Press.

Hervieu-Léger, D. (2000). *Religion as a chain of memory*. Polity.

Holroyd, J. (2019). *Judging religion: A dialogue for our time*. Silver Wood Books.

Hughes, B. (2015, August 5). *Genius of the ancient world: The Buddha*. BBC Four.

Jackson, R. (2014). *Signposts: Policy and practice for teaching about religions and non-religious worldviews in intercultural education*. Council of Europe.

Jaffrelot, C. (1996). *The Hindu nationalist movement and Indian Politics, 1925 to the 1990s: Strategies of identity-building, implantation and mobilisation (with special reference to Central India)*. Hurst & Company.

King, A. (2007). For love of Krishna: Forty years of chanting. In G. Dwyer & R. J. Cole (Eds.), *The Hare Krishna movement: Forty years of chant and change* (pp. 134–167). I.B. Tauris.

King, R. (1999). *Orientalism and religion: Postcolonial theory, India and 'The mystic east.'* Routledge.

King, R. (2008). Orientalism. In D. Cush, C. Robinson, & M. York (Eds.), *The Routledge encyclopedia of Hinduism*. Routledge.

Knott, K. (1998). *Hinduism, a very short introduction*. Oxford University Press.

Kurien, P. A. (2006). Multiculturalism and 'American' religion: The case of Hindu Indian Americans. *Social Forces, 85*(2), 723–741.

Lopez, D. S. (2002). Introduction. In D. S. Lopez (Ed.), *Modern Buddhism: Readings for the unenlightened* (pp. ix–xliii). Penguin.

McCutcheon, R. T. (2017). 'Is everyone religious?' and 'What is the future of 'religion'? In A. W. Hughes & R. T. McCutcheon (Eds.), *Religion in 5 Minutes*. Equinox.

McMahan, D. (2008). *The making of Buddhist modernism*. Oxford University Press.

McMahan, D. (2012). Buddhist modernism. In D. L. McMahan (Ed.), *Buddhism in the modern world* (pp. 159–176). Routledge.

Mukti, P. (1997). New Hinduism: Teaching intolerance, practising aggression. *Resource: Professional Reflection on Theory and Practice in Religious Education, 20*(1), 9–14.

Nai, P., Sun, J., Zhang, Y., & Yang, G. (2020). Religious education legislation in an atheist state: Towards a typology and policy analysis for contemporary China. *British Journal of Religious Education, 42*(1), 75–89.

Nye, M. (2001). *Multiculturalism and minority religions in Britain: Krishna consciousness, religious freedom and the politics of location*. Curzon Press.

Oberoi, H. (1994). *The construction of religious boundaries: Culture, identity and diversity in the Sikh tradition*. Oxford University Press.

Oddie, G. (2008). Hinduism. In D. Cush, C. Robinson, & M. York (Eds.), *The Routledge encyclopedia of Hinduism*. Routledge.

Prinya, N. K. (1996.) *Explaining Hindu Dharma: A guide for teachers*. RMEP/Chansitor.

Prinya, N. K., et al. (1998). 'New Hinduism' as seen by British Hindus. *Resource: Professional Reflection on Theory and Practice in Religious Education, 20*(3), 11–14.

Rahula, W. (1985). *What the Buddha taught* (2nd ed.). Gordon Fraser.

Radhakrishnan, S. (1948). *The Bhagavadgita, with an Introductory Essay, Sanskrit Text, English Translation and Notes*. Harper & Bros.

Reader, I. (1991). *Religion in contemporary Japan*. Palgrave/Macmillan.

Reader, I. (1998). *The simple guide to Shinto*. Global Books.

Rochford Jr., E. B. (2013). Sociological reflections on the history and development of the Hare Krishna movement. In G. Dwyer & R. J. Cole (Eds.), *The Hare Krishna movement: Forty years of chant and change* (pp. 11–35). I.B. Tauris.

Said, E. (1978). *Orientalism: Western conceptions of the Orient*. RKP.

Sharma, U. (2000). Book review of explaining Hindu Dharma: A guide for teachers. Norwich: RMEP/Chansitor. *Ethnic and Racial Studies, 23*(3), 617–619.

Sharpe, E. J. (1977). *Faith meets faith: Some Christian attitudes to Hinduism in the nineteenth and twentieth centuries*. SCM Press.

Smart, N. (1968). *Secular education and the logic of religion*. Faber & Faber.

Smart, N. (1999). *World philosophies*. Routledge.

Smith, J. Z. (1982). *Imagining religion: From Babylon to Jonestown*. Chicago University Press.

Smith, J. Z. (1998). Religion, religions, religious. In M. C. Taylor (Ed.), *Critical terms for religious studies* (pp. 269–284). University of Chicago Press.

Smith, W. C. (1978). *The meaning and end of religion*. SPCK.

Staal, F. (1989). *Rules without meaning: Ritual, mantras and the human sciences*. Peter Lang.

Taylor, R. L. (1998). The religious character of the Confucian tradition. *Philosophy East and West, 48*(1), 80–107.

Thapar, R. (1985), Syndicated Moksa? *Seminar, 313,* 14–22.

Vivekananda, S. (1994). *The complete works of Swami Vivekananda. Volume 1. Mayavati memorial edition*. Advaita Ashrama.

Wallis, S. (2014). Ticking 'no religion.' A case study amongst 'young nones.' *DISKUS, 16*(2).

Woodhead, L. (2016a). Changing religion, changing RE. *REtoday, 33*(2).

Woodhead, L. (2016b, January 19). *Why no religion is the new religion*. Talk given at the British Academy. https://www.youtube.com/watch?v=hPLsuW-TCtA

Ye, W., & Law, W.-W. (2019). Pre-service teachers' interpretations of religious policy in citizenship education in China. *British Journal of Religious Education, 41*(3), 327–336.

Zavos, J. (2008). Sanatana Dharma. In D. Cush, C. Robinson, & M. York (Eds.), *The Routledge encyclopedia of Hinduism*. Routledge.

CHAPTER 6

Teaching about Islam: From Essentialism to Hermeneutics

An Interview with Farid Panjwani and Lynn Revell, by Gert Biesta

Gert Biesta, Farid Panjwani and Lynn Revell

Abstract

This chapter is in the form of an interview undertaken by Gert Biesta with Farid Panjwani and Lynn Revell, exploring the problem of essentialism in the teaching of Islam in schools.

Keywords

essentialism – hermeneutics – Islam – interpretation – philosophical hermeneutics

Gert Biesta (GB):   In your work you have expressed a concern about essentialism in religious education, particularly around the teaching of Islam. Before we look at education, can you say a bit more about the representation of Islam more generally? Is essentialism an issue there as well?

Farid Panjwani (FP) and Lynn Revell (LR):   It is indeed a bigger issue. In fact, it is rare to find occasions when essentialism is not an issue in religious education as well as in societal discussions about religion generally. For example, consider how Islam is discussed in the media or in everyday parlance. Let's take a concrete example of essentialisation and then we can try and describe it. We often find claims such as 'Islam is ... x or is not x.' This way of approaching Islam, that is by postulating what it is or it is not, which, by the way, can be applied to other religions as well, is widespread. A search on the internet or a browse through school textbooks on Islam will show many examples: 'Islam is a religion of equality,' 'Is Islam

© GERT BIESTA, FARID PANJWANI AND LYNN REVELL, 2021 | DOI: 10.1163/9789004446397_007

compatible with democracy?' 'Islam is incompatible with moder-
nity' 'Are human rights compatible with Islam?' 'What is Islam's
view of other religions?' When we start the discourse about Islam,
or, again, for that matter about any religion, in this manner, we com-
mit ourselves to what has been called an essentialist understanding.
This framing forces us to seek an essence that defines Islam.

GB: How, then, would you define or describe essentialism?

FP & LR: Essentialism is basically the tendency to assume that a phenomenon or an idea has a set of characteristics which make it what it
is. Often this is accompanied by a further assumption that how that
phenomenon was in its original state, determines its essence. It is
like thinking that a river is only truly a river at the point of its origin.
In the case of Islam, for example, essentialism would mean that it
has a certain set of characteristics – beliefs, rituals, social relations –
which make it what it is and which are to be found in its origins, that
is in earliest texts and practices, the Qur'an and the Sira and, for Shia
Muslims, additionally, the words of the Imams. Consequently, later
ideas, perspectives, practices are seen as incursions or deviations
from the essence. It is, as if, to continue the river analogy, the water
at other places in the course of a river, in its conflux or in delta is
seen as less authentically river than the source.

GB: What is the problem when this happens?

FP & LR: There are ontological as well as consequential problems. Ontologically, essentialism commits reification – that is, it makes Islam,
which is an idea, into a thing, almost akin to a physical object.
Think of the question we looked at earlier, Is Islam compatible with
democracy? It is as it we are thinking of Islam as object and asking
for its compatibility with the equally essentialist idea of democracy.
Of course, even physical objects do not remain the same over the
course of their existence. Then there are consequential problems.
An essentialist understanding makes it hard to understand the
diversity within a religion, the different ways in which people actually experience, understand and practice Islam, or any other religion. One who carries an essentialist view of Islam is forced to think
of diverse forms as inauthentic. Such a boundary between Islamic
and un-Islamic can then easily transform into intolerance and, in
extreme cases, violence. There is an educational problem too. An

essentialist approach limits the ways pupils can understand and engage with the varied ways in which Islam has been understood and practiced in the past and present. Rather, they learn that there is only one way to be a Muslim. It constrains rather than nurtures autonomy.

GB: Can you say a bit more about that? And is it a particular problem for teaching about Islam?

FP & LR: Though the teaching of any religion can be a difficult task, in the current political climate, where fear of terrorism is routinely associated with religiously inspired violence, teaching about Islam can be particularly challenging. Islam was singled out as the source of the most dangerous contemporary ideology by Lord Carlyle in his report on UK terrorism laws, for example, and has since become the focus of security fears in a number of spheres. More problematically, the essentialisation of Islam can lead to an Othering, contributing to a political climate in which Muslims are often portrayed as the antithesis of the West and values associated with it.

GB: How would you say that Islam is being essentialised in RE?

FP & LR: Islam is essentialised in RE through a synthesis of a range of factors that can be observed in textbooks, examinations and agreed syllabi. Lack of diversity is often the simplest way in which essentialisation happens. This is beginning to change but still there is a long way to go. Take, for example, how, in many books, women with Muslim heritage are represented. In most cases, they are shown clad in a hijab. Similarly, the use of Quranic verses is often taken as a proof text without reference to multiple and contextual ways in which they are used in Muslim contexts. The categories through which Islam is presented in the curriculum means that the complexities and nuances of Islam as it is lived through Muslim communities is simplified so that diversity and difference between Muslim groups is blurred or presented as a deviation from its original 'pure' form. A recent research on RE, the project 'Does RE work?' (Conroy et al., 2013) found that there was a mutually reinforcing relationship between the way religions are presented by examinations and the agreed syllabi, online resources and textbooks. It is through these entrenched relationships that an essentialist model of Islam is articulated and sustained. This means that even where opportunities exist for teachers to explore diversity and difference within Islam they are often lost or are too transitory to make an impact on the dominant approaches to teaching in RE.

GB: Is this problem known in the literature? Amongst scholars? Amongst religious educators?

FP & LR: Though the tendency to take an essentialist approach to Islam has been strongly challenged in the academia and in scholarly works on RE, it continues to hold sway in schools, media, policy papers and even among sections of academic work. In scholarship on RE, for example, many works critique the essentialism of Islam and argue for an RE that gives pupils opportunities to engage in the varieties of religious life – which is also the point we have been making ourselves.[1] Many studies on Islam in education tend to reiterate the view that the teaching of Islam and the representation of knowledge about Islam in the curriculum are constructed in a context where many Muslim communities feel increasingly socially marginalised. But this critique is rarely reflected in the curriculum or resources. We are inclined to conclude, therefore, that Islam is actually systematically essentialised throughout difference aspects of RE. In her discussion of the idea of tolerance the political philosopher Wendy Brown (see Brown, 2006) has described how it is accepted that Western societies are complex and impossible to understand through the lens of one single category. In contrast societies in the non-western world are presented as simpler and comprehensible through simple characteristics or a single lens. In endless textbooks we can see the playing out of this narrative as adherence to the same markers (dress, beliefs, festivals, rituals) is identified as the defining characteristic of belonging to religious communities. Approaches to the teaching of Islam that define Muslims through a focus on essential, ahistorical features are in effect creating and legitimising a stereotype. This stereotype is then perpetuated in textbooks and materials that present the Muslim who regularly worships at a certain type of Mosque and who believes and interprets the Qur'an and key beliefs in certain recognisable ways as an ideal type. And even where diversity within Islam is recognised, it is represented within cultural silos so that 'different types' of Muslims appear as a series of stereotypes, the liberal Muslim, the extremist Muslim, the Pakistani Muslim, and so on.

GB: Does it also have something to do with the idea of Islam as one of
           the 'world religions'?

FP & LR: Definitely. Though the model of world religions is presented as a
           neutral model of religiosity that emphasises common themes,
           practices and beliefs among the worlds' great religions, it has been
           critiqued for ignoring the complexity and syncretistic nature of
           religious experience. It has actually also been shown to be a con-
           sequence of European universalism and a product of discourses on
           empire towards the end of the eighteenth century that conceptual-
           ised every religion through the categories associated with Christian-
           ity. By postulating that each of the world religions has a set of core
           beliefs, practices, and concepts that define and shape its essence,
           the model legitimises a 'hegemonic representation.' That means that
           essentialism not only presupposes that a particular group shares
           defining features that are common only to them but also, in the
           case of Islam, those features are created by a dominant discourse
           that privileges the values and practices of one religion over another.
           In the case of RE, the categories associated with world religions are
           actually rooted in Christian traditions so that the notion of a world
           religion, the prism through which pupils engage with all religions,
           is one defined by Christian religiosities. In the context of RE, essen-
           tialism others Islam through establishing a series of narratives, rein-
           forcing patterns of knowledge that create not just a stereotype but
           one which is defined by its difference from the cultural norm.

GB: There is a strong case then that Islam is being approached in essen-
           tialist ways throughout all levels of RE practice. Are there also criti-
           cal voices? How do they try to counter the essentialisation of Islam?

FP & LR: A common way to critique essentialist understanding of Islam is
           to point out to the actual practices and the diversity of Muslims.
           In this regard, cultural and doctrinal diversity are most prominent.
           The new exam syllabuses,[2] for example, require students to learn
           about doctrinal diversity among Muslims, as noted above. It is, how-
           ever, not clear that this focus on diversity is effective and sufficient
           in countering essentialism. A person holding an essentialist under-
           standing of Islam does not have to deny the presence of diversity—
           be it cultural or doctrinal. S/he can accept diversity and yet deny
           its validity by claiming that it is the result of misunderstanding the

'real' Islam and its teachings. It is often not recognised that it is not only groups such as Taliban and ISIL who deny the validity of diversity by insisting on a 'real' Islam, much of the reformist movements in Muslim societies – be it modernist or traditionalist – share this view, thereby seeking to find the original, real teachings of Islam.

For example, in the late nineteenth and early twentieth centuries, as Muslims were seeking to retain the relevance of sacred texts of Islam in modern times, essentialist approach was a key rhetorical strategy to achieve this goal. For instance, in his book, Ibtaal-e-Ghulami (refutation of slavery), Sir Sayyid Ahmed Khan (1818–1898), a well-known Indian Muslim reformer, argued that though slavery was common among Muslims of his time, it is contrary to the original spirit and teachings of the religion. In other words, in Sir Sayyid's view, slavery was not part of the real Islam but a mistaken practice that now needed to be abolished. You can see that this pattern of challenging existing Muslim practices by an appeal to original 'true' Islam continues in the reformist writings.

Similarly, when a modernist Muslim claims, for example, that the real teachings of Islam are compatible with modern understanding of human rights, and that those practices among Muslims that undermine human rights are therefore contrary to Islam, s/he is taking an essentialist approach, just as, of course, the person who claims that Islam is incompatible with human rights. Hence, it seems that pointing out the diversity of Muslims is not enough to challenge the essentialist reading of Islam.

GB: So how do you propose to tackle these issues?

FP & LR: We think that a better response to essentialism is to go further than simply present diversity. We need also to ask, why we have diversity of Muslims, and within religions, in the first place. We should help students understand that the diversity is not an add-on but a necessary feature of the way humans operate, make meaning and form traditions. We think this will help students resist the tendency to think about religion in terms of difference rather than by trying to eliminate differences and seek a monolithic or pristine understanding of Islam. To do this, we need to bring in the notion of hermeneutics.

GB: Can you say a bit more? Why is hermeneutics important here?

FP & LR: At the heart of hermeneutics is the question of interpretation – be
            it the question of interpreting texts or taking human understand-
            ing itself as inherently interpretive. Hermeneutics deals with a
            variety of issues. Literally, hermeneutics is about types of texts and
            processes of reading. Socially, hermeneutics is about social, critical
            or sociological questions about how vested interests may influence
            how we read. In linguistics, hermeneutics is about reception of texts
            and the impact of readers and communities.

            In most of its history, hermeneutics has largely been about tex-
            tual interpretations, particularly dealing with religious texts. In the
            twentieth century, however, especially under the influence of Hei-
            degger and more so Gadamer, a new understanding of hermeneu-
            tics emerged, called philosophical hermeneutics. It concerned
            itself not with the particular ways of reading texts but with human
            understanding and its interpretive nature. As Gadamer has pointed
            out, hermeneutics is not one of the ways in which human beings
            engage with the world around them; it actually is the very way of
            being of a meaning maker, which humans are. For Gadamer, then,
            hermeneutics is what he calls 'the basic movement of human exist-
            ence.' In other words, the process of making sense, of seeing some-
            thing as a chair, or hearing the sound of our name, already involves
            an interpretive process. Interpretation is inescapable, be it in the
            reading of a text or glancing at the face a friend.

GB: I assume this also counts for religion itself then?

FP & LR: Indeed. Let us approach this in concrete terms. Take a verse from
            the Quran such as verse 103, chapter 3. It reads, 'Hold fast the rope
            of Allah and do not become divided.' Even those who would wish
            to stay at the literal level will find it hard to do so here. Rope of
            Allah will require some interpretive element for it to make sense,
            since there is no physical rope to which this can refer. If we make
            it more complex and ask a question such as what does the Qur'an
            say about the relative status of men and women, the interpretive
            scope becomes immense. Here, there are many responses ranging
            from those who believe that the Qur'an prescribes absolute equal-
            ity between men and women to those who see men as superior
            to women and women as unfit for some tasks in life. All of these
            positions will appeal to the Qur'anic verses and claim authentic-
            ity. These are all exercises in interpreting the text, even though the

interpreters will often not see it as such. The diversity of positions on any issue, the range of rituals, the variety of beliefs are all result of interpretive processes in religious lives. The fundamental insight here is that the meanings of any text, understood in the broadest sense, are not in the text completely. Nor are the meanings imposed by the reader completely. Meaning is created; it emerges through a dynamic interaction which Gadamer calls the 'fusion of horizons' of the reader and the text.

GB: Can you say something more the 'fusion of horizons,' particularly in religious contexts?

FP & LR: Yes, sure. For Gadamer, fusion of horizons is about dialogue, say between a speaker and a listener or a reader with the text. In everyday use of the term, the horizon is as far as we can see or understand. For Gadamer it is the range of vision that is possible from a given position or a particular historical situation. At any given time, there is a limit to how far we can see, how much we can understand, how much we can envision. But, this limit is not permanent. It changes when we change our position, for example by moving to a higher physical space. The speaker and the listener, the reader and the text have horizons. But, these are indeterminate and can change. The dialogue allows for the expansion of horizons. Meaning is the outcome of this dialogical process of fusion of horizons. This fusion expands the horizon of both the reader and the text. The reader grasps perspectives it previously did not have, the texts reveal possible meanings previously not shown.

        Imagine a novel that you read at the age of 20. You come to the novel with some background and expectations and bring to it many competencies in language and reasoning as well as myriads of socio-cultural assumptions. These make up your horizon. But, the novel too has horizon. It belongs to its own linguistic, artistic and intellectual context. Upon reading the novel, you will make sense of it in some ways, reacting to it, making a judgement about it, identifying with characters or not, gaining insights or not about matters of importance to you. Suppose further that now aged 40, you come across that same novel. But, is it the same novel? In one way, it is the same novel – the physical text is identical. But, in another way, it is not. This is because you had read it earlier in a different context and perhaps remember, even vaguely, the sense and judgement made at that time. Hence, the novel is already a part of your horizon and your earlier reading of it is part of its horizon. We do not read the same text twice just like we do not put our hand twice in the same river. The text and its context as well as the reader and her context have both changed and upon re-reading the novel you may now react and respond very differently, or not. The outcome, what meanings, sense and judgement will be made, cannot be predicted. The same process happens with everyone who reads this same novel with myriads of outcomes in terms of meanings. As Umberto Eco observes 'A good book is more intelligent than its author. It can say things that the writer is not aware of.'

GB: Would you argue, then, that this is happening within religions such as Islam as well?

FP & LR: That is indeed the point we would like to argue for. This hermeneutical process, that meanings emerge in the dynamic engagement of text and reader, within the context of community, authority and tradition, is the basis of the diversity that we see within the Muslim tradition, or for that matter in any religious context. When people in Makkah first heard the message of the Qur'an, it led to a variety of response – from its acceptance to indifferent rejection to active opposition – depending upon the ways in which the texts fused with the historically situated beings of the people who heard it. And this process of interpreting the message and responding to it a range of ways has continued ever since.

GB: What does this mean for the idea of sacred texts in religions such as Islam?

FP & LR: When a child grows up in a Muslim context, s/he comes to accept the sacred character of the Qur'an even before reading it. In that context, the Qur'an is not just another text, though of course it is always a text. The child approaches the Qur'an with a pre-understanding of it as a divine text. The Qur'an does not become sacred as a result of reading it for the first time; rather it is read for the first time as a sacred text. The history of sacred texts is in fact the history of an ongoing fusion of horizons, of, on the one side, the range of sacred texts and the entire textual, and broadly religo-cultural tradition around them which includes the languages, commentaries, history of ideas, socio-political intellectual context and, on the other side, the diversity of people, the readers, the believers and their context which includes their background, intellectual and emotional makeup, socio-economic contexts, and historically affected conciseness. The continued fusions lead to the making of meaning in which both sides engage and shape each other and form the basis of resulting diversity in scriptural interpretations, theological orientations, political positions, moral persuasions and artistic appropriations.

Interestingly, it seems that the Qur'an is cognisant of necessity of interpretive activity. Take this verse from the third Surah, al-Imran: "He it is Who revealed to you the Book, in it are verses that are clear (muhkamat) – they are the essence of the book (Umm al-kitab) – and others that are allegorical (mutashabihat). Those in whose hearts is doubt pursue the allegorical seeking (to cause) dissension by trying to give explanations. And, none knows their explanation except God [...] And those who are firmly rooted in knowledge [...] say: 'We believe in them; the whole is from our Lord,' but only those with understanding really grasp" (Qur'an, 3:7). The first part of the above verse divides the Qur'anic verses into those that are clear and those that are allegorical. But, the verse does not tell us how to distinguish between the two. This decision is left to the reader. Next, though the reader is not told how to distinguish between the two types of verses, pursuit of allegorical verses has been discouraged. Similarly, the very last part of the verse calls for an interpretation, as depending on where the stop sign is put, the section can be read in two very different ways.

GB: So there is really work for the reader to do, then.

FP & LR: Indeed. Let's take a more concrete example. It is often asked, what is Islam's attitude towards other religions. Note the essentialist formulation of the question. An obvious way to respond will be to say that the answer can be found in the Qur'an. But, if we will turn to the Qur'an, we will not find an unequivocal answer. Instead we will find a variety of attitudes towards Jews and Christians ranging from that in verses 2:62, which creates a bond among people from different religions that rests on faith in God and good deeds, transcending particular theological positions and identities, to that in verse 5:51 which admonishes Muslims against taking Jews and Christians as their friends. These different attitudes reflect the changing nature of relations between neophyte Muslims and Jews and Christians of that time, but they leave Muslims with the task of engaging in hermeneutical activities to work out which attitude they ought to take today.

GB: Are there limits to interpretation? Or does it all hang on how crea-
           tive readers are?

FP & LR: The short answer is both a yes and a no. Yes, because there is no
           limit to interpretations, except the readers' creativity in coming up
           with plausible ones. However, the hermeneutical approach is not
           just about a reader reading the text. It situates the act of reading
           in a tradition of a community of readers and the nature of author-
           ity in that community. So, the text, tradition and the community
           put limits to what is accepted as legitimate interpretation at any
           time. Not everything goes. There are always boundaries put to
           what counts as acceptable. These limits can vary from community
           to community. In some communities there are narrow limits as to
           who can be a Muslim. In others, the limits can be very broad. But,
           and this is important to note, these boundaries are at a given time
           only and do not put limits to the possible future interpretations.
           That which was deemed Islamic at some point (say slavery) can
           become un-Islamic at another point; that which is un-Islamic today
           may become Islamic tomorrow. It is in this sense that we can say
           that Muslims make Islam as much as Islam makes Muslims. And,
           let me add, since Muslims share the world with everyone else, their
           own understanding is shaped by that wider context and what is said
           about Islam in it.

GB: How important is all this then for where we started our conversa-
           tion, that is with rather strong claims about what Islam is and what
           it is not?

FP & LR: Let us take an example of a claim about Islam, that it is a religion
           of peace. As we know, there is the counter claim too, that Islam is
           a religion of violence. These are both strong and essentialist claims
           about Islam. Now, the vast majority of Muslims believe and have
           a coherent theology of peace drawing upon the Qur'an, the life of
           the Prophet and other sacred sources. But, there are also Muslims
           who believe in militant fights and wars in the name of Islam, again
           drawing upon the verses of the Qur'an, elements from the life of the
           Prophet and other sources. Believers in each of these claims gener-
           ally think that Islam is inherently what they believe it to be. But,
           if we step back, it should be clear that both of these claims have
           been Muslim constructions. Hence, when we ask about Islam, we

should realise that we are indeed asking about how Islam is understood by Muslims. And, this, in turn, opens up other questions: why do Muslims understand Islam differently, what is the role of the context, of particular traditions and inclinations of the readers? So, we deepen our understanding of the text as well as of what Islam, or a particular belief, means for a woman or man, what it means for a person to follow Islam. As Bowen (2012) notes, this places an increased emphasis on religious texts and ideas, but only as they are understood and transmitted in particular times and places.

GB: So if we look at essentialism from a hermeneutic perspective, what, then, is the problem with essentialism?

FP & LR: We think that essentialist approaches do not do justice to the religious text, in that they do not recognise their openness and capacity to produce new meanings; to the religious people in that it makes them a passive recipient when in fact they are actively engaged in the meaning making process; to the histories of a religious tradition in that it does not recognise its diversity, dynamism and contested nature.

GB: Can you, in conclusion, draw some pedagogical implications for teaching Islam hermeneutically?

FP & LR: There are several. At one level, it suggests that we change the questions we ask. Instead of asking, for example, What is Islam's conception of knowledge?; or: What is Islam's view on Christianity? WE should ask, 'how have Muslims understood the concept of knowledge in light of their religious texts/traditions?' Or, 'how have Muslims understood Islam's relationship with Christianity?' This form of question reorients the answer to social actors, their uses of texts and tradition, the processes of meaning making and the broader social contexts in which these takes place. At another level, it can help redress a problem in the presentation of Islam and that is overemphasis on rituals, doctrines and legal prescriptions and prohibitions. Not enough attention has been paid to other ways in which Muslims have made meaning and expanded the idea of being Islamic: the artistic, the philosophical, the mystical and the literary. Exposure to these ways of making meaning allows the students to engage with a whole range of ways in which Muslims have seen themselves to be so, from those who define Islam in legalistic terms to those who venture in mystical and poetic explorations and from those who think of Islam as their primary identity to those who while retaining some form of Muslim, if not Islamic identity, lead secular lives and think through most of life's problems and challenges by means of a secular worldview.

GB: And what would it entail for students?

FP & LR: Firstly, it helps students, regardless of their own background and orientation, to gain insights into the complex ways in which meanings are made by the believers resulting in the internal diversity that seems to be a feature of all religions. An understanding of the study of religion in schools that engages with what Aldridge (2015) calls a 'hermeneutical sensitivity' is certainly one that allows the possibility of different interpretations. Secondly, for those students who also belong to religious traditions, in this case Islam, it can be autonomy enhancing as they will see that religions continue to remain relevant through the interpretative acts of believers and that, in their subjectivities, they too can participate in this process. Thirdly, as the meaning making processes are not restricted to producing morally good and sanctified acts of believers, it allows for a more historically sound presentation of a religious tradition whereby controversial practices, interpretations and outcomes can also be explored without ascribing these to religion per se but seen as a part of a religious experience of humankind.

GB: Thank you very much.

Notes

1   See, for example, Panjwani (2005); Revell (2012).
2   This refers to the standardised public examinations taken in England at 16 and 18.

References

Aldridge, D. (2015). *A hermeneutics of religious education*. Bloomsbury.
Bowen, M. (2012). *A new anthropology of Islam*. Cambridge University Press.

Brown, W. (2006). *Regulating eversion*. Princeton University Press.

Conroy, J., Lundie, D., Davis, R., Baumfield, V., Barnes, P., Gallagher, T., Lowden, K., Bourque, N., & Wenell, J. (Eds.). (2013). *Does religious education work?* Bloomsbury.

Panjwani, F. (2005). Agreed syllabuses and unagreed values: Religious education and missed opportunities for fostering social cohesion. *British Journal of Educational Studies, 53*(3), 375–393.

Revell, L. (2012). *Islam and education*. Trentham Press.

CHAPTER 7

On the Precarious Role of Theology in Religious Education

Sean Whittle

Abstract

This chapter focuses on religious education in Catholic schools to argue that despite first impressions, theology plays a precarious role. It presents an analysis of what theology typically involves and then argues that this reveals how, in religious education, there a serious under emphasis on the living faith that underpins the academic theology that is part-and-parcel of these lessons. Through drawing on insights from Biesta and Hannam it is proposed that the role of theology in religious education is to raise the consciousness or awareness of children and young people. This will help them to know and understand how living the religious life well is a desirable way of being a grown up in the world.

Keywords

theology – revelation – Catholic religious education – faith – transubstantiation

1 Introduction

To suggest that the role of theology in religious education is precarious, might on first impression appear counter-intuitive. Indeed, it is not uncommon for schools, especially Catholic ones, to name the subject 'theology.' Moreover, when advertising for teachers of religion a premium is often put on finding theology graduates. A widely held assumption is that the curriculum subject religious education shares a tangible relationship with the academic discipline of theology found in many universities. This would mirror the relationship between other parts of the curriculum, such as geography and mathematics. This chapter challenges this assumption at a number of levels, beginning with difficulties in pinning down what actually counts as theology, in order to argue that the role of theology in religious education is indeed currently shaky and uncertain. This is a problem for children and young people because they do deserve to encounter a rich theology as an integral part of their religious education. Moreover, it will be maintained through drawing on the arguments developed by Biesta (2017) and Hannam (2018), that teachers would need children and young people to engage with central aspects of theology as a fundamental part of their religious education. The failure to include it would impair the goals of education and do a profound disservice to children and young people.

In what follows I will be working with the analysis that Biesta has developed over a number of years (2012, 2014, 2017) which draws attention to the unhelpful over-emphasis on learning, which he describes as the problem of 'learnification,' and the need for a renewed emphasis on the significance of teaching – as an event. It is through a 'rediscovery of the significance of teaching' that education is able to find a way out of the impasse caused by overstating the significance of learning. Biesta (2017) demonstrates how reconsidering the role of teaching allows some fundamental questions about the goals of education to fall into sharp focus. Fundamentally, teaching needs to go beyond learning, to engage with questions about what does it mean to exist as a grown up in the world. Teaching has a pivotal role in fostering the desire to exist in the world in a grown-up way. All parts of the curriculum (where teaching occurs) have a role to play in this, including in religious education. The question thus morphs into how can religious education foster and support this kind of desire in children and young people? This question frames another, about what is it that the religious education teacher is seeking to teach. In teasing out the answer to these questions the role of theology will become clearer. However, before doing this it is necessary for some qualifications to be drawn and for some ground clearing to be done.

2   Setting the Context and Clearing the Ground

First, the context for the broader argument to be developed in this chapter is firmly anchored in a Catholic Christian context. To begin with, I am writing this as a serving religious education teacher, drawing on my experience (over two decades) of working exclusively in Catholic schools in the UK. In addition, the conceptual stances taken towards the nature of theology reflects a typically Catholic Christian one. Thus, what is being presented is the position of one Catholic religious education teacher rather than a definitive Catholic analysis. Thus, from the Catholic school stance the opening assumption of this chapter is that religious education is heavily loaded with theology.

The content of the religious education curriculum in England and Wales in Catholic schools, which is normally given 10% curriculum time, is specified by a document known as the *Religious Education Curriculum Directory* (2012). The most extensive section of the directory is found in Part III (pp. 10–52) which focuses on the areas of study. This part specifies the content of religion lessons, from nursery through to Sixth Form level. The content of religious education is organised into sections which correspond to four of the central documents promulgated at the *Second Vatican Council* (1962–1965). This organisational structure is used to present the content of religious education lessons. Throughout these four sections a sequence of summary statements, of five or six sentences in length, is followed by a number of single sentence statements drawn from Catholic doctrine, for example about 'revelation,' such as 'The nature of revelation: God's gift of himself' (*Religious Education Curriculum Directory* (2012, p. 13). Each of these statements is numbered and then proceeded by a list of other ones drawn from Catholic belief and doctrines. Typically, these lists contain five or six statements. These supporting statements contain references to the *Catechism of the Catholic Church* (1992). In total there are over 1,300 statements which form the content of Religious Education lessons in Catholic schools. At the theoretical level, thanks to the *Religious Education Curriculum Directory,* theology is presented as integral or built into the very structure of religious education in Catholic schools.

At the practical level in Catholic secondary schools, thanks to the dominance of the GCSE RS course – which all students are compelled to take – a generous portion of theology is very much part-and-parcel of religious education lessons. It is widely recognised that the 2016 revision of GCSE examination courses resulted in content heavy specifications across all subjects, and this certainly is the case in the Religious Studies qualification. Typically, in Catholic schools the specification followed requires students to wade through topics which are full of theological doctrines and underpinned by cross references to the *Catechism of the Catholic Church* (1992), scripture and citations from magisterial Church teachings. The companies who administer the public examinations have tailor-made specification subsections that comply with the *Curriculum Directory* for use by Catholic schools. Critical evaluation is a major component of the RS GCSE specification and this is built into the kinds of questions poised in the examination questions.

As a consequence of this, some of the demands made of the students are highly complex, such as evaluating the relative strengths and weaknesses of the theological metaphors about whether or not the Church ought to be primarily understood as the 'body of Christ' or as the 'people of God.' This is a challenging question within ecclesiology to ponder through, let alone resolve.

Indeed, it is not actually clear that it is a theological dilemma that stands in need of resolution. Moreover, with the requirement that two religions be examined, young people at Catholic schools are also engaging with Jewish (or in a few schools, Islamic) theology.

Thus, both at the theoretical and practical level, theology already has a key role to play in religious education in Catholic schools. Perhaps a case could even be made for arguing that it is actually overburdened with certain types of theology. Paradoxically students have adapted well to the increased theological content and appear to be soaking it up with some skill. The initial two sets of results for the post 2016 RS GCSE specification remain very strong, with many Catholic schools boasting significant proportions of students getting the highest level possible. In some Catholic schools, performance in religious education outperforms all other subjects at GCSE.[1]

Although at the surface it would appear that the role of theology is far from precarious in Catholic schools, there are some signs that this might not be the case at the more fundamental level. Much of this is to do with the way theology is presented and used, especially within the GCSE RS course. In Chapter 8 of this volume, Bowie raises concerns about the adversarial characteristic built into the structure of many of the RS GCSE exam questions. The focus in these types of question is on presenting theological stances in binaries and rewarding students who can 'win' in analysing or resolve the purported theological dilemma when evaluating them. This is linked with the use of scriptural citations or Church doctrines as proof texts which can be used to trump what appear to be competing theological claims. There are also other concerns with the way theology is being characterised within religious education in Catholic schools. Notably, theology is being characterised as very much an intellectual pursuit. This fosters the idea that there are theological arguments that can be 'lost' or 'won.' Whilst this might be reminiscent of the scholastic theology of the Middle Ages, which featured theological disputations, it bears no real resemblance to the way Catholic theology has been framed and conducted from the middle years of the Twentieth Century onwards. Indeed, the proceedings of the Second Vatican Council, 1962–1965, are taken to be a decisive rejection of the neo-scholastic (legalistic and adversarial) and anti-modernist approach to theology that dominated the first half of the twentieth century – and in fact much of the post-Reformation period (Alberigo, 1987).

In addition, it can be argued that the way Catholic Christianity is characterised theologically in RS GCSE is in what Panjwani and Revell (see Chapter 6) would describe as 'essentialist.' Whilst their analysis is in regard to Islam, the same case can be readily made for Catholic Christianity. Thus, the complexities and fine distinctions of Catholic Christianity as lived by real communities of people tends to be ignored. Just as Islam is often treated through exam syllabi or textbooks in an essentialist way (see Panjwani and Revell in chapter 6), a parallel case can be made about the way Catholicism and its underlying theology are treated. Theological doctrines frequently get treated in ahistorical ways and this can lead to stereotypical accounts in religious education of what it is to be a Catholic Christian.

One way to illustrate this is to consider the doctrine of transubstantiation in relation to the Eucharist. In religious education lessons this can all too easily be presented along stereotypical lines about all Catholics accepting the coherence of the underlying Aristotelean physics, eschewing any attempt to couch it as in any sense symbolic or within a richer sacramental theology. The focus of the lesson can become fixated around the need to both accurately assert and assent to the doctrine of the 'real presence.' This is to cast the theology of the Eucharist in an overly technical frame in which it becomes vulnerable to naïve or literal interpretations. This dogma of Catholic Christian faith too readily falls into a binary issue – of accepting or rejecting the 'real presence.' To reject it or perhaps even question it, is to step outside what might be considered as orthodox Catholic belief. Unfortunately, teaching about the theology of the Eucharist in this way leaves aside a broader and richer exploration of the place of the Eucharist – in particular about receiving Holy Communion – for Catholic Christians. Abstract and intellectual discussion of transubstantiation and the real presence have little, if any connection to the lived reality of the place of the Eucharist for Catholic Christians. The issue here comes down to the relationship between theology and faith. This issue needs some careful teasing out and is bound up with a second part of the ground-clearing, around unpacking how best to characterise theology.

3   So What Counts as Theology?

The multiple levels of meaning associated with theology frequently fail to be unpacked and fully recognised. Already in this chapter, reference has been made to 'Catholic dogma' and underlying 'Catholic theology.' This usage is clearly presupposing that theology has denominational variants. Unfortunately, appeals to the etymology of theology, with its roots in the Greek concepts of *theos* and *logos,* bring us just to a fairly uninformative 'words about God.' In the twenty-first century an uncontroversial observation is that theology applies to a cluster of overlapping disciplines and social practices which have deep roots and traditions. From a western university perspective, theology is the broad intellectual pursuit or subject areas that typically include biblical studies (Old Testament/Jewish scripture, Inter-Testamental studies, and New Testament studies), systematic or dogmatic theology (focusing on God, Jesus, Salvation, Revelation and Ecclesiology), historical theology (patristic theology, reformation theology, missiology/world Christianity), sacramental theology, moral theology, catechetics, feminist theologies, liberation theologies, Church history and pastoral theology.[2] There are schools of thought in theology (such as Thomism, scholasticism and neo-scholasticism).

One of the prime characteristics of the denominational variants of the theology is the relative waiting and ordering of these branches of theology. For example, protestant theology typically prioritises biblical studies, in particular the New Testament, and treats the remaining branches as significantly inferior or having to be filtered and interpreted in the light of scripture. In recent centuries a large swathe of protestant theology has adopted a hermeneutical stance of fundamentalism and biblical literalism. Another debate surrounds whether or not pastoral theology ought to be viewed as a peripheral albeit practical application of other parts of theology or considered as central or at the heart of all theology. The priority of pastoral theology would appeal to teachings from the early days of the Jesus movement about love in action; loving your neighbour as yourself because in the least of your neighbours God will be found. For the Abrahamic religious traditions, a similar clustering of disciplines can be identified, and given this it makes sense to refer to Islamic theology and Jewish theology. At the boarders of theology there is the emerging discipline of inter-religious dialogue which stands alongside the more established field of religious studies. The Wittgenstein metaphor of a family resemblance can be helpfully applied between theology and religious studies.[3]

On top of these levels of complexity there are further distinctions that can be drawn in relation to the connections between the discipline(s) of theology (as framed from a Western university setting) and the faith of Christians. The Christian faith, as it is lived out in practice within communities of people, shared customs, beliefs and values is of course underpinned by theology. For example, when Christians gather, their prayer and rituals will be framed in a Trinitarian format (praying *to* the Father, *through* the Son and *in* the Holy Spirit). Similarly, scriptural texts are regarded as the *Word of God* rather than simply much-loved bits of literature. Following Anselm of Bec in the Eleventh Century, a frequently used definition of theology is that it is 'faith seeking understanding.' Implicit in this definition is that theology is a second order activity, coming after or in support of the faith that a believer already holds in response to the God who reveals. Drawing on this kind of distinction between faith and theology opens up some important possibilities. The first is about potential dissonances between the living faith of Christians and the discipline(s) of theology (to say nothing of individual theologians and differing theological schools). The second is the possibility that theology could be undertaken by people who do not share the faith. It is intriguing to note the way university faculties in countries like the UK will now readily market their theology courses to potential students as primarily academic activities which do not presuppose a faith commitment. Thus, the notion of an atheist theologian (as opposed to the student of theology who has lost their faith) cannot be regarded as an incoherent one.

Of course, the distinction between faith and theology pivots on the way faith is primarily understood. The range of synonyms for the term 'faith' typically include trust, belief, confidence, dependence, conviction, reliance and hope. At the etymological level the concept of faith is rooted in the Greek *pistes* and Latin *fiducare*. These differing roots have allowed two dominant meanings to emerge.[4] The first characterises faith as a stance of loyalty or commitment to some person or cause. The second puts the emphasis on assenting to a set of beliefs, having faith in the beliefs specified or identified, normally by others from a position of authority. Frequently these differing meanings have become conflated. In relation to theology, the ambiguity or conflation around the meaning of faith is perhaps what has made the space for the tension in Anselm's definition of theology as faith seeking understanding. There is also an echo at play of the debate about whether or not pastoral theology is at the centre or periphery of theology.

In the light of this ground-clearing, it becomes easier to see why, despite first impressions, the role of theology is in a perilous state in religious education in Catholic schools. The prime reason is to do with an over emphasis on theology as an intellectual pursuit that draws on just some of the disciplines that typically constitute the subject (at university). The task of religious education is to teach and learn about the beliefs and values that Catholic Christians are supposed to assent to – if they are to be regarded as orthodox believers. However, this is a deeply risky or perilous stance because it ignores the ways in which theology is a second order activity to the faith of living Catholic Christians. For children and young people, the danger is that this sort of religious education turns the faith of believers into an object of study that comes down to an investigation and evaluation of the range of beliefs that are supposed to be held. This is the mistake of making a second order analysis more important than attending to the first order reality, about the nature of the faith people hold. The theology that is currently part of religious education deals with the technical and surface level theology (for example, around transubstantiation) rather than the more fundamental level of lived out faith (for example about why receiving Holy Communion means so much for most Catholic Christians).

Thus, the role currently played by theology is perilous because it has the danger of either seriously misrepresenting or just ignoring what Catholic Christian faith involves.

Of course, the advantage of the current role played by theology in religious education is that it is more amenable to assessments and the testing regimes that schools use to provide formal qualifications. Testing students about a range of beliefs and using citations from scripture or dogmatic statements as proof texts is far more straightforward to assess than delving into the living faith of real people who belong to a Church community. Another advantage is that it avoids the longstanding concerns about confessional education in religious education (Hirst, 1972). Just as theology can be pursued as an academic discipline, innately intriguing within itself, without the need for personal faith, the same is true of the young people in religious education lessons. The issue of the child or young person's faith or lack of it can thus become an irrelevant issue in religious education. Moreover, there is a well-established argument from Arthur (1995) that Catholicity (the Catholic faith) has been ebbing out of Catholic schools over many decades and is now all but gone. This fuels a contemporary caricature which depicts a situation in many Catholic schools where religious education is now taught by non-believing theology graduates to young people who are encouraged to study the subject in a way that ignores any faith they might have or encounter in the course of these lessons. The religious education they are engaged with is in effect regarded as a scaled down version of the theology taught at university. For some, such as Robinson (2017), who is a national advisor for religious education in English Catholic schools, the subject is primarily an academic activity, in which key tenets of Catholic theological tradition are taught to young people to ensure that they have a good knowledge and understanding of it. Ultimately this is to present children and young people with an impoverished engagement with theology.

4   Enhancing the Role of Theology in Religious Education

An intriguing question is how best to respond to the precarious role that theology currently plays in religious education in order to place it on a firmer footing. The motivation for doing this is precisely because children need an enhanced engagement with theology as 'faith' seeking understanding, in order to be adequately educated. One quick response is to argue for the need for both increased time and a greater exposer to more of the branches of theology. Given the complexity and richness of theology, the real problem facing its role in religious education is that young people are not getting enough theology to properly engage with it. Young people deserve a far richer selection from the disciplines that make up theology. By appealing to a metaphor that likens theology to a grand cathedral, it is only by stepping in and exploring all of the architecture and taking time to appreciate the grandeur of the structure that one comes to know and grasp what the cathedral is all about. Thus, it is only by opening up more of theology through allocating a greater proportion of curriculum time to religious education that young people can get a better grasp of theology. This argument might have some purchase outside of the Catholic sector, because of the insufficient curriculum time devoted to religious education. The *Final Report* of the Commission on RE (CoRE, 2018) presents a stark analysis of just how many schools fail to give religious education even minimal time. However, in England and Wales, for Catholic schools a hefty ten percent of all curriculum time is typically devoted to religious education lessons. Thus for these schools there is no shortage of time to fully explore the cathedral.

5   One Way Forward

Although elsewhere I have made the case for a reimagined account of religious education as part of a non-confessional theory of Catholic education (see, Whittle, 2014), the focus in what follows is to outline another possible way forward, drawing heavily on Biesta (2017) and Hannam (2018). As a starting point, it is important to recognise that the cogency of Biesta's position is taken as a given in what follows and will not here be subjected to scrutiny. Instead the attention is on explaining how it suggests a framework for reappraising the educative place of religious education.[5] Once this is clarified, it will be possible to reconsider what the role of theology in religious education is best taken to be.

   To begin with Biesta, argues against prioritising learning when considering the fundamental questions of education. Instead attention ought to be given to the place of teaching as a way of fostering in children and young people the desire to exist in the world in a grown-up way. In contrast, an infantile relationship with the world puts the child's desires central and involves a failure in the child to recognise that she is a subject which stands in relation to the world – and the other subjects in the world. A grown-up way of being in the world recognises that one is a subject in a world which contains other subjects. Both the world and the curriculum place demands on the child. A grown-up attends to these demands and is able to respond to them in a way that does not prioritise oneself. The teacher, through teaching the subjects of the curriculum, has the pivotal role in fostering in the child or young person being taught the desire to exist in the world in a grown-up way, as a subject or being in a world which makes demands on them. Framing teaching in these terms makes it possible for teachers to raise questions about how their given subject has a role to play in fostering this desire. For the teacher of religious education, a primary question is about how religious education can foster and support this kind of desire in children and young people.

An answer to this is for religious education to be attentive to what it might mean for a grown up to live a religious life well. There are of course a range of different ways to live in the world as a grown up. However, it is for the religious education teacher to help children and young people to make sense of what living the religious life well involves. Almost inevitably this would require that in religious education it is a priority to understand the place of faith in the religious life. This would necessitate exploring how a living faith involves a loyalty to and relationship of trust in God. There is a wide agreement that living the religious life well involves something of what Kierkegaard described as the 'leap into faith.' The emphasis is on a relationship of trust and openness to the transcendent. As Kierkegaard's metaphor draws out, this relationship is not something one investigates with an academic interest, rather it is something that is leaped into. A religious education that explores what it means to live a life where making a leap into faith makes sense, is one which puts the role of theology on both a firmer footing and a different trajectory. The attention in religious education is firmly on the nature of the living faith held by real communities of people. This is to attend to the first order activity, rather than to prioritise the theology which has unfolded in seeking to make sense or understand faith.

It is important to tease out a bit further the implications for religious education in a Catholic school. The priority is no longer on gaining a grasp of some of the many branches of theology, but rather the more fundamental theological claims within the Catholic Christian faith. These are about engaging with the possibility of being a grown up in the world who is addressed by God who is revealed in the human being Jesus Christ. Coming to attend to what it is to live this religious life well would guide and inform the content of religious education. Almost inevitably this means religious education will make it possible for young people to explore and attend to what this leap into faith as a Catholic Christian might involve. It will be about being attentive to what a life built around an ongoing relationship with God (through Jesus) might mean for a grown up being in the world. The crucial role of the religious education teacher is to raise the consciousness or awareness of children and young people. This will help them to know and understand how living the religious life well is a desirable way of being a grown up in the world. Of course, their other teachers will be making them attentive to alternate ways of being a grown up in the world, and what is desirable about these. All those involved in teaching children and young people have a role to play in making them aware of the freedom needed for the leap into faith to be made. Teaching, as Biesta suggests, might provide a highly apt role model for children of what the leap into faith involves. This is because teaching actually involves making a leap into faith concerning the child: "as teachers we orient our actions towards that which is not visible in the here and now – the student's subject-ness – which is a matter of seeing what is not visible" (Biesta, 2017, p. 94). It is interesting to speculate that if there is to be the rediscovery of the significance of teaching that Biesta has advanced, all teaching might end up supporting a key goal of religious education. Teachers through the event of teaching could be role-models who live out the leap into faith.

Whilst this approach to religious education is attractive, it has so far avoided the issue of confessionalism. Of course, many of the concerns about confessionalism stem precisely from worries about the appropriateness of engaging children and young people with living religious faiths. In order to safeguard autonomy and to guard against even tacit indoctrination there has been a deep reticence about the way faith is taught or opened up to children in formal education settings. In responding to the threat of confessionalism there are two quick responses. The first is to dismiss it as a false dilemma, because there are no neutral spaces or worldviews from which a child or young person can engage with religious education. The second is to argue that the grounds for confessionalism are often heavily overstated, not least because the issues are more theoretical and are unlikely to occur in practice. Advocates of Catholic education are often quick to point out that Catholics schools are particularly ineffective at indoctrinating and unsuccessful at ensuring children practice their faith into adulthood (Whittle, 2014). However, it may well be these quick responses are not enough to avoid the concern over confessionalism. Thus, teasing out how this reframed account of the role of theology in religious education is to adequately avoid even tacit confessionalism needs further attention.

6   Conclusion: Theology and Education

The thrust of this chapter has been to demonstrate how theology can be rescued from the precarious role it currently faces in religious education in Catholic schools (and all schools). This has been achieved through drawing on the insights of Biesta surrounding the rediscovery of the significance of teaching. By way of conclusion I want to re-echo Biesta's observation (see Chapter 1) that this analysis is actually indicative of a more fundamental relationship between theology and education. This is because in reappraising the activity of teaching, as an event, what also comes into sharper focus is an affinity between the movement or structure of both revelation and teaching that occurs in education and life. This affinity can be explained in these terms. Teaching disrupts the infantile or egocentric ways of being that characterises the child or young person, by bringing them to attend to aspects of the world which come to them whether it is wanted or not. The student is presented with what is other to herself, through the phenomenon of teaching. Similarly, revelation is disruptive of our ways of being in the world. The theology of revelation pivots on it being God's initiative and outside of the wants or actions of human beings. God reveals as God reveals and as such it is for us to deal with and respond to. Thus, the structure of teaching and of divine revelation are the same. The affinity here is not confined to the teaching that goes in religious education. It repeatedly crops up through the entire curriculum. However, in practice it may well be that it is only in religious education lessons that this fundamental connection between theology and education is drawn out and named.

Acknowledgement

I am indebted to Professor Dr. Bert Roebben for both the title and initial stimulus for the arguments developed in this chapter.

Notes

1   See for example the GCSE results for Gumley House Convent School in 2019.
2   Alongside universities, seminaries and theological colleges would add to the range of disciplines to also include others such as liturgical studies, homiletics and Canon Law.
3   Denise Cush presents an analysis of the tensions which exist between religious education, theology and religious studies (1999).
4   For a more comprehensive discussion of this see Hannam (2018).
5   A sophisticated and highly coherent use of Biesta's relevance for religious education has already been developed by Hannam (2018).

References

Alberigo, G., Jossua, J.-P., & Komonchak, J. A. (Eds.). (1987). *The reception of Vatican II.* Burns and Oates.

Arthur, J. (1995). *The ebbing tide: Policy and principles of Catholic education.* Gracewing.

Biesta, G. (2012). Giving teaching back to education. Responding to the disappearance of the teacher. *Phenomenology and Practice, 6*(2), 35–49.

Biesta, G. (2014). *The beautiful risk of education.* Routledge.

Biesta, G. (2017). *The rediscovery of teaching.* Routledge.

Catholic Bishop's Conference of England and Wales. (1992). *Catechism of the Catholic Church.* Chapman.

Catholic Bishop's Conference of England and Wales. (2012). *Religious education curriculum directory of Catholic Schools and Colleges in England and Wales.* Catholic Education Service.

CoRE (Commision on Religious Education). (2018). *Religion and worldviews: The way forward. A national plan for RE.* Final report. Religious Education Council of England and Wales. Retrieved April 3, 2020, from https://www.religiouseducationcouncil.org.uk/wp-content/uploads/2017/05/Final-Report-of-the-Commission-on-RE.pdf

Cush, D. (1999). The relationships between religious studies, religious education and theology: Big brother, little sister and the clerical uncle? *British Journal of Religious Education, 21*(3), 137–146.

Hannam, P. (2018). *Religious education and the public sphere.* Routledge.

Hirst, P. (1972). Christian education: A contradiction in terms? *Learning for Living, 11*(4), 6–11.

Robinson, P. (2017). Finding purpose in Religious Education. *The Tablet, 271*(9199). https://www.thetablet.co.uk/supplements/13/9892/finding-purpose-in-religious-education

Whittle, S. (2014). *A theory of catholic education.* Bloomsbury.

CHAPTER 8

Implicit Knowledge Structures in English Religious Studies Public Exam Questions: How Exam Questions Frame Knowledge, the Experience of Learning, and Pedagogy

Robert A. Bowie

Abstract

This chapter is not so much a critique of an exam, as an analysis of religious education (RE) through a study of the principle question structure used in exams, and the kind of answer responses that can become norms. It examines implicit knowledge structures that implicitly prefer binary argumentation rather than nuanced and contextual discussion, literalism and proof-texting with sacred texts rather than polyphonic multidimensionality and contextual readings, and contradictory rather than compatible differences. The question structures in exams assert a kind of knowledge in RE constructed by and for examinations. For the most part, they do not test disciplinary knowledge and forms of religious knowing have no recognised place.

Keywords

examinations – argumentation – proof text

1   Investigating Religious Education through Its Exam

This chapter is not a criticism of examinations per se despite its title. A principal aim here is to identify the habits of practice in answers to these questions that score points but in bad ways making reform of the Religious Studies GCSE exam, which over 200,000 students take in English schools, at around the age of 16, desirable. The GCSE is the most sustained and significant effort in English formal education in religion, taken by most students, and so it is crucial for the subject of religious education as a whole.

© ROBERT A. BOWIE, 2021 | DOI: 10.1163/9789004446397_009

To seek to address this problem in an exam discussion has merit. First, in English state-funded schools, exams, in general, have a very high prominence in secondary schools. They matter in instrumental terms to school performance measurement (a big aspect of English schooling). They have a significant impact on the secondary curricula as a whole. Exams reach back through the school curriculum to the extent that 11-year old's arriving at secondary schools are made familiar through practice with the questions they will face at 16.

Second, exams play some part in the future available destinations for students in terms of further and higher study. They reach up out of the school, framing how a subject is perceived.

Third, as relatively high-status moments in an educational life, they offer a concentrated highlight of the subject to a broader public. There is a general concern about what sorts of things students get tested on. In English religious education recent history, a principal example of this was the move to require all exams to cover two religions which came from a general political, and social view of the benefits of study of more than one religion during the Conservative-led Coalition government (2010–2015), under Michael Gove as Secretary of State for Education.

The exam frames the classroom experience, in so far as the curricula lead to the exam as a summation, but it does not exhaust it what teachers do with an exam specification matters to the overall experience. The resources, techniques and approaches they adopt to engage with the requirements are not identical though standardised approaches are developed by professionals. Exam knowledge may not be all that a subject 'gives' to a student and problems within exams may not be replicated in the understanding held by students. To move from a 'question problem,' to a presumed more magnified problem is a transition that is difficult to evidence definitively.

However, a suggestion that all of the problems identified in this chapter are corrected in classroom settings is unrealistically optimistic without a sufficient body of analysis of actual written answers and classroom observations. This chapter itself lacks a sustained analysis of the actual answer provided on scripts or a generalizable systematic analysis of all of the features of professional practice bearing on these answers which is far beyond the scope of what is possible in a book chapter. However, the norms of practice embedded in the textbook design, in online social media professional groups, is strongly suggestive of a parallel between this analysis and many teacher's experiences.

For any subject area, the exam questions and specification organisation should marry well enough with the subject area. There should be a correlation between what is tested, on the one hand, and what matters in the subject, on the other; Both in terms of the various kinds of knowledge and skills associated with a subject and its disciplines. Questions should sustain this marrying and not unduly distort. However, there is undue distortion brought about by the most important mark bearing question. The exam contains questions of different kinds, but long answer questions have half of the marks. They are designed to show analysis and evaluation through a discussion and debate. The debates may be ethical, philosophical, theological or sociological.

These long answer questions tend not to require the demonstration of specific disciplinary knowledge in their structuring, apart from a general philosophical or sociological inductive and deductive argumentation approach with arguments sustained by reasons and evidence and reference with sources of authority (not simply unevidenced opinions). It would be possible to draw on textural hermeneutics, theological understanding, psychological understandings, anthropological understandings or other theories of religious studies. However, the knowledge of these areas is not part of the explicit curriculum studied, and the tools they offer are not mainly tested, beyond basic argumentation.

2   Background

Previously I argued with Richard Coles (2018) that the English Religious Education exam system (Religious Studies GCSE) had systems and structures that not only permitted but encouraged poor use of bible texts in student answers. That research was based on two studies: one of the exam questions and another of the Exam board examiner reports and textbooks. It was built on a body of research and reports that pointed to problems related to how the Bible was engaged in the classroom over at least 20 years (Bowie, 2018, 2019). What was striking about that research was the repeating pattern of some of the problems over time, indicating that they have become deeply integrated within RE.

The most recent form of the exam uses a particular type of question, which we pejoratively and provocatively called the proof text binary argumentation question, constitutes half of all marks in this exam. It prescribes the role of sources of wisdom and authority (commonly quotes from sacred texts). The poor use of sacred texts long reported in research and other reports continues. Perhaps the only advantage is that students would learn banks of quotes and at least know these quotes.

Beyond the relatively small number of students who take an option in a Gospel paper since the recent GCSE reforms of 2014 (perhaps 2.5% of the total student body), the encounter with sacred texts is about the questions that require a proof to back up a point of view. While there might be a desire for students to use texts in ways that reflect their interpretation and use by Christians, this is not directly a focus. The curricula do not start with the question, 'what are the ways in which religious people reflect on their experience of faith and life,' but with a focus on a belief or practice and how a text relates to that way.

The principle purpose of texts in these questions is a reasoning justification in an argument about behaviours, attitudes, practices or beliefs. The long answer question is a critical focal point as it draws together all of the skills tested by shorter questions but with an evaluative dimension. It is not the only kind of question, but it represents a high point of engagement given at the pinnacle position in all GCSE exams irrespective of the board as it carries half of all marks. The new specifications have an increased emphasis on these questions, so preparation for these questions is a key part of teaching and learning in GCSE Religious Studies classrooms.

This long answer question has traditionally been used in exams to explore issues of contention that are commonly moral or about points of religious practice. Pupils need to show knowledge and understanding of these arguments and an ability to structure that knowledge in a long body of writing. The most recent evolution in the question has tried to make that debate more informed with an emphasis on sources of authority due to the specific concerns identified in RE reports (Ofsted, 2007, 2010, 2013) mirrored in the review of examiners reports above. These questions crystallise the implicit aim of teaching students to conduct a reasoned debate and come to a conclusion. The nature of the reasoning and the use of any disciplined approach in that reasoning is not proscribed.

Here are a couple of recent examples of these questions.

'A loving God would not send anyone to hell.' Evaluate this statement. In your answer, you should:
– refer to Christian teaching
– give reasoned arguments to support this statement
– give reasoned arguments to support a different point of view
– reach a justified conclusion.
Page 4. 1B/M/Jun18/8062/13. Monday, May 14 2018, GCSE Religious Studies A Paper 1 Christianity. AQA.

'Infant baptism is not as important as believers' baptism.' Evaluate this statement. In your answer, you should:
– refer to Christian teaching
– give reasoned arguments to support this statement

– give reasoned arguments to support a different point of view
– reach a justified conclusion.
Page 4. Monday, May 14 2018, GCSE Religious Studies A Paper 1 Catholic Christianity. 1B/M/Jun18/8062/12. AQA.

'For Catholics, the best way to serve God is by helping the poor.' Evaluate this statement. In your answer, you should:
– refer to Catholic teaching
– give reasoned arguments to support this statement
– give reasoned arguments to support a different point of view
– reach a justified conclusion.
Page 9, Monday, May 14 2018, GCSE Religious Studies A Paper 1 Catholic Christianity. 1B/M/Jun18/8062/12. AQA.

'Evangelism should be the most important thing for Christians today.' Discuss this statement. In your answer, you should:
– Analyse and evaluate the importance of points of view, referring to common and divergent views within Christianity
– Refer to sources of wisdom and authority.
[15 Marks] Spelling, punctuation and grammar [3]
(OCR, 2016)

3   Seven Features of the Implicit Structure of Knowledge in the Proof-Text Binary Argumentation Question

My aim here is to develop in much greater depth the framing of religion that takes place by the use of questions of this kind and show what the shaping influence of an exam can be. It shows the reach an exam can have in constructing the knowledge within a *kind* of worldview with a *version* of a disciplinary knowledge structure that proscribes what religion is and also how it is best studied.

3.1   *Fragmentalisation*
The proof text binary question encourages the fragmentalisation as the principal focus of discussion is an application of a text to an argument or topic. The focus is not the text as such, not the narrative of the big picture in which a quote sits, so any reference will most likely be to the fragmentary 'source of authority'. It is quite likely that students will learn banks of questions as part of their revision. They have been taught that these quotes link to the issue, and

the curriculum is a collection of issues. It sets the encounter with the religious worldview as one with extracted nuggets. The frame of view reduces a worldview to bite-sized bullet points which can be used to win an argument. Perhaps this would be acceptable if there was an established systematic understanding of the operation of a worldview as a narrative-led reality reading system. That hope might be better secured in most or all classrooms if exam questions required the location of a quote in the richer narrative around the source of the authority referred to given the centrality of the Bible to Christian life. While that could be achieved in answers to the existing questions, it would still be a second-order objective.

3.2   Decontexualistion

It necessarily requires decontextualistion of sacred texts to be used to serve the interests of the question setting and answering. It is difficult, though not impossible, to imagine answers to these issue questions, having space for how the reading of text makes meaning in the broader narative tradition. The context is the debate that the quote is required to be placed in. Quotes in the debate are the focus and ultimately, what will be rewarded. Of course, these sacred texts do get drawn into debates in a decontextualised form, but within the worldview which holds them sacred, they are also situated in other multiple contexts. In Christian worldviews, they will commonly be located in collective liturgies/worship, in personal lives of prayer, in the retelling of the wider sacred text narratives, not to mention the historical development of the text and the multiple readings of that text in the development of theological ideas.

An adjustment to the question structure could encourage better behaviour with these two areas such as 'Explore different approaches to how sources of authority are read and interpreted' for instance. This would still not allow for a substantial analysis of a text using the ways of knowing and reading sources of authority, but at the very least it would focus attention on discussions around the use of texts in argumentation.

3.3   Propositionalisation

Because of priority given to the text as a source, or reason for a belief it implicitly preferences the propositionalisation of religion, the representation of religion to a series of propositions held up by texts. A student studying this course will need to know the beliefs and practices held up by sources so they can be repeated on request for the examiner. Worldviews can be understood as collections of propositions, both by the people who hold a propositonally framed worldview, and also by those who view all worldviews to be essentially propositional structures. However, propositional religion is a particular framing. There are also significant examples of religion as praxis/practice, and symbolic and existential understandings of religion. Religion as something akin to way, being, doing or habitus. Religion, as *doing and being*, is less compatible with the propositional structure, and so the question format preferences propositional religion. Propositionalisation invites a particular frame for thinking about religion that suits philosophical debate but has been rejected by the religious themselves (for instance, in the Catholic Churches rejection of Hume's definition of miracles). In combination with decontextualisation and fragmentalisation, propositionalisation is most likely to lead to an emphasis on religious literalism and, in a debate, this is likely to then set up a pattern of religion as literalism vs the rejection of religion as literalism. At a most reduced level, this paves the way, conceptually at least, to the foundational binary as fundamentalism vs atheism. This suits those who seek to win a debate, and those who privilege that *particular* debate.

3.4   Positionalisation

It encourages positionalisation, the portrayal of religion as taking *a view* from which other positions are to be opposed. Positionalisation has been elevated by the recent discourse around worldviews in the English religious education system. There are good reasons to question whether religion or worldview should be framed as a view from a point. There is a teleological focus within the dimensions that should be included in the study of religion which establishes some directionality, but perhaps this is not important enough to be the main, let alone mostly exclusive, focus. Taking encourages an adversarial as we take positions *against* other positions.

Propositionalisation and positionalisation serve argumentation and debate. They are essential features of the question style.

3.5   Normalising Contrasting Diversity

The question structure normalises contrasting diversity as the essential focus of study with the implicit encouragement of the teaching of extremes as these are easier to refer to, to demonstrate that difference is known. Showing difference as opposites in a confrontational 'boxing match style' comes to dominate the classroom experience of RE. Contrasting diversity is valued more highly in this question structure than coherence or integration. A student answer that shows a detailed analysis of complex integration of different elements, even contradictions, would be in danger of losing diversity. Yet integration and coherence is a principal structural feature of religion.

Contrasting divergence is privileged as an indicator of higher criticality and complexity, but analysis and interpretation are inadequately considered as a result. These are servants to winning the argument in the current structure. There is here for a progressing normative relativism which is amplified by the requirement to show knowledge of opposites in arguments, rather than any other particular justification.

3.6   *Difference as Divergence Rather Than Multi Layeredness*
The normative concept of difference is mainly understood as divergence rather than multi layered-ness Non-oppositional difference is undervalued, and binarism is overvalued. This is a serious error as forms of religion commonly have layers of meaning within cooperating structures, which include, for instance, symbolic, pragmatic, intellectual and historical layers of sense. Teachers can draw these out in their teaching, of course, but the incentives for doing so would be enhanced by question structures which encouraged their exploration. This seems particularly grievous to scriptural narrative traditions which commonly contain multi layeredness.

Difference as divergent opposition suits the fundamentalist – atheist hypothesis that you must choose between one or the other of mutually excluding positions. This is RE as radio buttons study.

This results in a number of difficulties, not least for those who wish to promote an open and diverse plural society. It promotes an essentialist idea that humans adopt one stance or another (rather than slipping between both or holding both simultaneously). Contrasting difference and difference as divergence are readings of reality held by those in positions that have a vested interest in the conflict hypothesis or the conflict itself. It links *being different* with *being a problem* and both of those things with *being religious*. It also implicitly suggests that humans do not hold within them contradictions and life does not require contradictions as well.

3.7   *Conflict Studies*
The overall result of this process is that the most sophisticated organising structure of the study of religion for most young people in GCSE exams is one that places conflict at the heart of the knowledge studied, at the expense of analysis of complexity, integration and coherence. While conflict is part of religious experience, focusing mainly on conflict misses the extent to which religion seems to address something which commonly groups find a shared experience of addressing. Should conflict take the highest point – the subject's pinnacle of knowledge? This is undoubtedly a profoundly secular reading of religion, where religion is a problem, and religious education is the study space of this problem. There are conflicts around aspects of life which involve disagreements of religion and worldviews, and while these are prominent in

popular culture and philosophical development, it is entirely possible that it is life that offers humans problems and that these problems are challenging to solve and, for those we cannot solve, are challenging to live with. It the organisation of the exam, *making sense of things* equates to *sorting things out*.

Several things can counter contrasting diversity, difference as divergence and conflict studies. Questions could make a requirement to show how different beliefs might reach shared understandings and overlapping interests in collective action, a feature of religions and interfaith cooperation. A specific emphasis on the contextual differences of different communities would also provide space to show adaptability within religious traditions rather than internal conflict. Difference need not lead to binary opposition. Difference might be a result of a sophisticated contextualisation, rather than an illogical incoherence.

4   Conclusion

Argumentation is vital as religion is a matter of differing beliefs, and so it would be possible that a student can posit anything as being true without the requirements to refer to sources of authority. From 'the outside' the secular perspective is of differences, divergences, and diversity and attention inevitably become drawn to instances where those trends lead to problems. However, this is a partial perspective. If a subject seeks to reach a deeper understanding of the religious life, then the features of coherence and integration of that way of life deserve focused attention. This requires a close analysis not only what is done or believed, but the way things are seen and known within religious life. The way of knowing matters.

The absence of a proscribed particular disciplinary knowledge, in theory, enables a multi-disciplinary approach allowing for a variety of knowledge organisations or argument scaffolds. However, the option of a broad range of choices permits several problems. First, because the question structures do lean toward certain argumentative forms of study including both positivistic philosophical and some socio-scientific constructions (such as Marxist and Freudian critiques of religion). This follows a particular linear narrative history of the discipline that theology led to a rise of the social sciences as a rejection of theology.

They lean away from spiritual/mystical, theological, ethnographic and anthropological constructions. Implicit disciplinary decisions have been made in the question design, which has consequences when a non-matching disciplinary approach is taken, teachers encounter difficulties.

Perhaps there needs to be a space in the school curriculum for students to be encouraged to debate but framing RE in that way has consequences. This implicit framing in the GCSE Religious Studies exams as inductive and deductive argumentation has led to practices associated with the exam questions and resulted in particular use of sacred text becoming common. This is the use of quotes as proof texts to sustain arguments, without associated familiarity with sacred texts scholarship. There is a characterisation of the subject as a study of disputes and disagreements. Texts are characterised as reasons for disagreements.

1. This kind of argumentation privileges what Cooling and others (2016) have called Christian positivism (texts and dogmas are proofs that can be used to argue for or defend the Christian worldview).

2. They privilege secular, atheistic positivism (logical arguments which disprove religious truth claims).

The privileged binary positivist structure is conjoined with a relative hermeneutical desert in the curriculum. Scripture scholarship and philosophical hermeneutics are not part of 'the knowledge that is taught'. The grammars of religious meaning and the kinds of significance that people hold are skewed into only those that function within positivistic constructions of the adoption, maintenance or defence of worldviews. As a result, there is a third damming consequence:

3. Symbolic interpretation, necessary for many aspects of religious knowing, is partly or entirely absent. Associated multidimensional areas of development and insight, be they spiritual, sacramental, personal, have insufficient space for development.

Put more simply, 'debate' is privileged over the maps of meaning that religious people and communities have developed to focus on what they hold to be significant. Although the exam is, in theory, emphasising analyses and evaluation, deductive and inductive argumentation define the kind of analysis and evaluation permitted and that which is excluded.

Quotes are being learnt to bolster arguments. Inevitably these short texts will be dislocated from context, outside of narrative or story, extracted beyond questions of intention, authorial purpose, historical resonance and theological and symbolic significance. This question form requires the demonstration of a "logical chain of reasoning" (AQA, 2016, p. 10) but this is not exclusively for philosophical or ethical topics but is being used for theology and religious practice. It preferences reasoning and debate rather than (for example) exegetical analysis or theological reflection. An analysis is included only in so far as it services the of winning of arguments (Cooling et al., 2016). Teachers are implicitly directed to encourage students to learn how to build chains of arguments for justified points of view, providing evidence underpinnned by sources of authority. The question expects students to rehearse arguments and engage texts as carriers of meanings to justify (preferably oppositional) positions in an argument with one another to reach a justified judgement, constituting evaluation. These essential features of the proof text binary argument question are not well suited for all kinds of religious content and serve the examination of religious texts badly, limiting the contribution religious studies courses can make to the development of students' capacities to interpret religion. It places logical reasoning at the heart of the enquiry in religion faith and life, things which might also, or be better characterised by reflection on paradox and mystery. Religious and spiritual traditions variously recommend as pathways for enquiry skills such as hermeneutics, attentiveness, contemplation, meditation and reflection, forms or enquiry which have little or no place in these assessments.

References

AQA. (2016). *GCSE religious studies a 8062/1A and 8062/1B the study of religions papers 1A and 1B mark scheme 2018 Specimen* [Online]. http://filestore.aqa.org.uk/resources/rs/AQA-80621-SMS-ADD.PDF

Bowie, R. (2017). Stepping into the text: How the Jesuits taught me to read the bible. In A. Voss & S. Wilson (Eds.), *Re-enchanting the academy* (pp. 139–155). Rubedo Press.

Bowie, R. (2018). Interpreting texts more wisely: A review of research and the case for change in English Religious Education. In J. Shortt & R. Stuart-Buttle (Eds.), *Christian faith, formation and education* (pp. 211–228). Palgrave.

Church of England Archbishops' Council Education Division and the National Society. (2014). *Making a difference? A review of religious education in 537 English schools* [Online]. Retrieved March 29, 2017, from https://www.churchofengland.org/education/publications.aspx

Conroy, J., Lundie, D., Davis, R., Baumfield, V., Barnes, P., Gallagher, T., Lowden, K., Bourque, N., & Wenell, K. (2015). *Does religious education work? A multi-dimensional investigation.* Bloomsbury Publishing.

Cooling, T., Green, B., Morris, A., & Revell, L. (2016). *Christian faith in English church schools: Research conversations with classroom teachers.* Peter Lang.

DfE. (2015). *Religious studies GCSE subject content.* Crown.

Fancourt, N. (2017). Teaching about Christianity: A comparative review of research in English schools. *Journal of Beliefs and Values, 38*(1), 121–133.

JCQ CIC. (2017). *GCSE full course by age UK* [Online]. Retrieved March 29, 2017, from http://www.jcq.org.uk/examination-results/gcses/2016/gcse-full-619 course-uk-by-age-2016

OCR. (2016). *GCSE (9-1) religious studies J625/01 Christianity; Beliefs and teachings & practices; Sample question paper.* Author.

Ofsted. (2007). *Making sense of religion.* HMSO.

Ofsted. (2010). *Transforming religious education.* HMSO.

Ofsted. (2013). *Religious education: Realising the potential.* HMSO.

CHAPTER 9

What Should Religious Education Seek to Achieve in the Public Sphere?

Patricia Hannam

Abstract

In this chapter I make a case for religious education taking an interested position in relation to action in plurality. Outlining how the public sphere, as well as how religion itself, are conceptualised, my argument develops through emphasising that religious education should make an educational contribution to education in the public sphere. Therefore, education's relationship with the public sphere is also explored here. Bringing this together, I show some new possibilities surface for religious education, where education is seen in relation to bring the child to action in plurality, rather than reason alone. In outlining these new possibilities, I aim to make visible the significance of including the existential response to what it means to live a religious life for the public sphere.

Keywords

religion – education – public sphere – action – religious education

1 Introduction

There has been a year on year rise in reporting of religiously oriented hate crime in England (Home Office, 2019). This is alongside clear documentation of the rise in xenophobia across the UK and especially against Muslims and Jews.[1] The UK is not alone in this; many European countries are also watching a rise of the Far Right including in France, Germany and Hungary. Given that not all European countries have a statutory obligation to provide non-denominational religious education for all in state schools, in some ways then, it is perhaps strange that this is happening in England despite compulsory religious education from the time children enter school at 4 years of age, right up to the age of 18. The 1988 Education Act put a National Curriculum in place for all subjects in England for the first time but excluded religious education in public schools. Instead it reemphasised that the creation and monitoring of religious education syllabus was the responsibility of regional government, known as Local Authorities, in England. This continued a system regarding religious education more or less as it had been since the 1944 Butler Education Act. Indeed, the Education Act of 1996, School Standards and Framework Act of 1998 and Education Act of 2002 each make clear that religious education should be taught to all children, according to an Agreed Syllabus that should reflect the fact that the traditions in Great Britain are in the main Christian, while taking account of the teachings and practices of the other principle religions in Great Britain. Further, legislation makes it clear that an Agreed Syllabus (agreed locally in each Local Authority) must not be designed to convert pupils, or to urge a particular religious belief on pupils.

It has been noted in several reports into religious education in recent years, that something is not going as well as it should be in schools. The All-Party Parliamentary Group (2013) Report on Religious Education, as well as Baumfield and Cush (2013), suggest religious education is at something of crossroads. Further reports published in 2015 (see, for example, Clarke & Woodhead, 2015; Dinham & Shaw, 2015) identify religious education as being most likely to contribute positively to developing 'religious literacy.' Calls for knowledge and understanding of religion to be included in public education have also been made in Europe (see for example Council of Europe, 2007; Davis & Miroshnikova, 2013) and have been discussed more widely (see for example Arweck & Jackson, 2012; Conroy et al., 2013; Baumfield, Cush, & Miller, 2014; Chater & Castelli, 2017). The Commission on RE Report (2018) calls for a 'new national plan' for religious education proposing among other things a change in the name from religious education to 'Religion and Worldviews,' hoping that this together with other legislative changes will make things better.

In this chapter I intend to offer something new to the discussion through following a line of enquiry that gives explicit attention to both constituent elements: religion and education. I do this because it seems possible that in much of what has gone on before, certain assumptions have been made about religion as well as what education itself should achieve. I hope to bring to the surface an option for religious education at this point in history that may have, as yet, been missed or at least under considered in other contemporary debates. The enquiry here may, at first sight, appear to be quite theoretical. However, I am optimistic by the end of the chapter I will have enabled the reader to appreciate the significance of its practical application, bringing clarity with regard to what religious education could be envisaged as doing in the public sphere.

My argument develops, with Simone Weil and Hannah Arendt, first by explaining how I understand the public sphere and then with a brief discussion about religion, in practical terms. I then offer some consideration as to what education should aim to achieve in the public sphere and, in the concluding sections I propose a contingent response to the question forming the title to the chapter. This leads me to the point where a further question becomes apparent as to whether religion may even have something particular and of value to bring to education. This is at least where what it is to live life with a religious orientation is conceptualised in existential terms, rather than only in terms of belief and practice. I close by asking whether religious education, that includes religion conceptualised in existential terms, may be able to make the difference between a group of people merely being in the same place at the same time and them existing together in the public sphere. And whether this is what has been missing in what has gone before.

2   The Public Sphere

Before proceeding, I should explain what is intended in this chapter by 'public sphere' and its relevance to the discussion. I acknowledge pre-existing distinctions between 'confessional' religious *instruction* that may happen at home as well as in religious community contexts and religious *education* in non-faith contexts in publicly funded schools. However, I also want to make a broader point about the relationship between religion and education politically. It has been noted elsewhere that religion is of political concern (see, for example, Schreiner, 2013). Further it is acknowledged that this has had a bearing on religious education internationally, at least since the publishing of the *Toledo Guiding Principles on Teaching of Religions and Beliefs in Public Schools* (OSCE/ODIHR, 2007). The Toledo Principles are "based on a human rights perspective that relies on OSCE commitments and international human rights standards" (p. 27). Indeed, interest in the relationship between politics and religious education has come about across Europe largely because of the emphasis on human rights since the Second World War. The Organization for Security and Co-operation in Europe (OSCE), an organisation founded in this period, has as its goal to work for stability, peace and democracy for more than a billion people across the region. With 57 member organisations internationally, it works through political dialogue advancing shared values, and through practical work it intends to make lasting difference. The Office for Democratic Institutions and Human Rights (ODIHR) is based in Poland, Warsaw and is the OSCE's principal institution to assist participating States "to ensure full respect for human rights and fundamental freedoms, to abide by the rule of law, to promote principles of democracy and [...] to build, strengthen and protect democratic institutions, as well as promote tolerance throughout society" (1975, Helsinki Document).

Tragic events such as September 11, 2001 in the USA also raised the international profile of religion. However, an exploration of recent debates (see, for example, Gearon, 2013; Jackson, 2014a, 2016) reveal a conceptualisation of the relationship between religion and education placed in the domain of politics and as being understood in relation to political structures and policy. Schriener, in emphasising that this is the case, has pointed out that "the political dimension of religion has become a decisive dimension of European policy" (Schriener, 2013, p. 5). Furthermore, and as Berglund, Shanneik, and Bocking (2016, p. 9) have noted, research in religious education itself has also tended to be characterised by a kind of 'methodological nationalism.'

In beginning to lay out my argument here, I bring a critique of too simplistic an account of the relationship between politics, education and religion and religious education through a reading of Hannah Arendt's understanding of the 'public sphere' (see, e.g., Arendt 1958, 2006) For Arendt, the reduction of human relationships in the world to narrowly defined institutions reveal an insufficient, and indeed she would say dangerous, conceptualisation of the political or public realm of human life. So, it is at the outset of this chapter, I want to make clear that the public sphere I am interested in is, as is Arendt, one that can actually exist in the world under certain conditions, and not simply remain an abstract idea(l). Arendt points out that just having a bill of rights or international declaration, even with the backing of a court of law, is not sufficient to secure the public sphere. If people lose the capacity to act (in the public sphere) despite being recognised as a 'man' this person will have lost the means by which to "make it possible for other people to treat him as a fellow-man" (Arendt, 2004, p. 381).

So it is that in this chapter I am not primarily interested, as others have been, in structural relationships between human rights and religious education. This is the kind of relationship well exemplified in the REDCo Project where The Toledo Protocol and its desire to promote tolerance, is linked with religious education (see, for example, Weisse, 2010; Jackson, 2011). Rather, I am more interested in how religious education, in educational terms, may be able to secure the conditions under which we could recognise the "disturbing miracle contained in the fact that each one of us is ... unique ..." (Arendt, 2004, p. 382). I hope to make clear why this is of importance to us all in the public sphere of life, and why it cannot be relegated to private concern. In Arendt's view the whole "sphere of the merely given (such as human rights), relegated to private life in a civilised society, is a permanent threat to the public sphere, because the public sphere is as consistently based on the law of equality as the private sphere is based on the law of universal difference and differentiation" (Arendt, 2004, p. 382). The key intention of this chapter is to consider how, as it relates to education, her position on the public sphere has something new to bring to our considerations of religious education and what it is understood to be able to achieve.

3   Reconceptualising Religion

In this section I take forward a discussion where religion is considered in practical terms. This is not where religion is conceptualised in abstract terms to be studied objectively, but in relation to different ways in which it is possible to respond to questions of what it means to exist, that is to live a life, with a religious orientation in the world. In brief I propose three responses to this question: each structurally different from the others. In the first case, being religious is seen not only as a matter of having beliefs, but also as asserting them to be true. This can be exemplified by considering Christianity which has had since the earliest times creedal statements. The second response to the question sees being religious as a matter of practice. This can be exemplified by considering Judaism, since it is possible to argue that for many Jews, what it is to live a Jewish life can be understood as conducting one's life according to certain rules or traditions. As discussed in more detail elsewhere (see Hannam, 2018, p. 87), this can be the case without ascribing to a set of beliefs, at least not if beliefs are only understood in propositional terms. The third response sees religion in terms of existence, meaning that living a religious life is a way of "being aware and leading one's life" (Hannam, 2018, p. 87). It is this third way of responding to the question of what it means to live life with a religious orientation that has been missing explicitly in many if not most documents regarding religious education that I mention in the introduction to this chapter. Simone Weil helps considerable in bringing clarity to the distinctions I want to make here, especially in her exploration of 'faith' (see, especially, Weil, 1965). Weil's exploration brings the subjective experience and indeed existence of each person into closer focus.

Theoretically, part of the difference I want to highlight here hinges on different possible translations of the Greek word 'pistes.' With regard to the first conception of what it means to live with a religious orientation, the Greek can be translated as 'belief' in the propositional sense. However, in the third conception it can be translated as 'trust' (Hannam, 2018, p. 87). A point I make here is that both, indeed all three, are important. However, if the existential and subjective sense is omitted from how living life with a religious orientation is conceptualised in religious education, something will be missed. As Weil enables me to make clear, and I will draw on later in this chapter, living a religious life where religion is understood as faith in existential terms will be qualitatively different from where religion is only understood in terms of propositional belief. The danger facing religious education if religion is only understood in terms of belief of tradition, is that such beliefs or traditions can become objectified and distanced from the ones holding them. Further and in light of this, there is a risk that the study of religion itself becomes only an examination of these beliefs or traditions in an objective sense, losing it connection from both unique human beings as well as the public sphere itself.

4   What Should Education Seek to Achieve?

My next step is to consider what education in the public sphere should seek to achieve at this point in time. Here, building on the discussion in the first section of this chapter, the word 'public' signifies not only the physical location of civic education, but refers to the quality of social action and interaction that takes place in the name of 'education' whether it is provided by the state or otherwise. In order to make a start on this I look to another point of crisis in human history in the 20th century, following the Nazi holocaust, and to some observations and reflections from Arendt. It may be helpful for those new to her work to appreciate something of Arendt's context, beginning with her escape as a Jewish woman from Nazi Germany, making her home in the US after ww2. At this point she looked back and puzzled how it could be that people like Heidegger, and other highly educated people, colluded with and supported Hitler and the Nazi project? *The Origins of Totalitarianism*, published in 1948, was written against this backdrop alongside a growing awareness of events in post-war Stalinist Russia. *The Human Condition*, published ten years later in 1958, was an investigation into the paradox of how, although our human powers increase due to technological and humanistic inquiry somehow, we seem less (not more) equipped to control the consequences of what we do.

In 1963 she was asked by the New Yorker Magazine to travel to Jerusalem to observe and write about the trial of Adolf Eichmann, published later as Eichmann in Jerusalem: A Report on the Banality of Evil. Arendt was disturbed by the process that led to the decision of the court to sentence Eichmann to death. What she saw was a man whose defence was that he simply did as he was told. He did not personally kill anyone; he was just doing his job – making the trains run efficiently. Arendt concluded that evil was not something somehow located in individual people. It was not simply a kind of quality, ascribable to them and capable of being destroyed were that person to be destroyed. Rather, in her view, evil is something that is enabled to arrive into the world when people do not think and therefore when people neither speak nor act for themselves. The condition under which thinking, and speaking are possible she had already begun to spell out in *The Human Condition*. This she explains is possible through 'action in plurality.' Her key point is that when people are not permitted, or in some other way not able, to speak and think for themselves the public sphere ceases to exist. And it is under these circumstances that totalitarianism can emerge.

By action, Arendt does not mean simply the range of different activities human beings do in the world. Instead action has a very particular meaning explained in large part by the clear distinctions she makes between this and two other ways human beings can exist in the world. That is between action and work and labour. Work and labour are the kinds of things that human beings do to keep themselves alive; growing food, making shelters as well as to make more beautiful things like tables and chairs or even flutes and violins. However, both work and labour are the kinds of activities that can be undertaken by ourselves without others; and for this reason, therefore cannot be the very particular and especial things that distinguish us as human. Both work and labour can be de-humanised and be de-humanising (think of production lines, or even Auschwitz). However, action is the kind of thing that must be undertaken with others; that is in plurality and where our uniqueness as human beings (rather than just abstract concept on 'man' or 'men') is revealed. It is action such as the way we speak and think together, that is she suggests, in plurality that is the miracle that can save the world.

The point I want to take forward here is that if public education is "aimed at fostering and maintaining interaction 'across difference,' with an orientation towards the democratic values of equality, freedom and solidarity" (Biesta, 2013, p. xiv), then action in plurality, in the Arendtian sense, should be understood also as being significant in education. This is not only because action is precisely concerned with the quality of social action and interaction between people, but also that action in plurality makes possible the recognition of the miracle of each unique human life. Arendt is interested not only in the miracle that marked each of our births into the world, but at least as significantly also in how, in each moment each of us is in a way born anew. This is as we emerge into the flow of every new moment in time in the world in the places beyond our homes. In other words, it is action in plurality that makes the public sphere possible.

This is the connection I want to make, proposing that education in the public sphere should take an interested position in relation to action in plurality. I argue against the 'common sense' view of education being primarily or even solely about the cultivation of reason (see Hannam, 2018, p. 76). As I will go on to show in the section of this chapter that follows, such an emphasis on reason is likely to lead to particular value being given to objective phenomena of religion. Further, that such phenomena understood in terms of knowledge in the propositional sense. This in turn can lead to emphasis in religious education in particular being given to epistemological questions, diverting away from educational concerns. Although this argument is part of a far longer one and explored fully elsewhere (see Hannam, 2018, pp. 70–86), I hope to be able to make clear why this way of looking at things might matter.

5   What Should Religious Education Seek to Achieve?

Through what has been so far discussed in this chapter, I can now propose that religious education, intending to make a contribution to education in the public sphere, should take an interested position in relation to action in plurality. New possibilities surface for religious education, where education is seen in relation to bring the child to action, rather than reason alone, and I'll attempt to sum them up simply in a few outline points through the rest of this chapter. In outlining these new possibilities for religious education, the significance of the existential response to the question of what it means to live a religious life becomes visible.

The key point is that where the existential is included, the task of religious education becomes one of bringing the child to be interested in the question of what it means to live a life, one with a religious orientation or otherwise, for themselves and for the world. No longer is religious education an objective study of propositional beliefs or traditions of others. Instead, beginning with the experience of the child or young person, opportunities are made for them to become interested bit by bit in all manner of ways human beings live in the world. Where religion is understood in existential terms, religious education can properly allow space for the child's own experience to be significant in the classroom. This idea is taken up and discussed in more detail educationally in Biesta's chapter earlier in this book, making clear the necessity of the child or young person who is being educated being at the centre of the educational discussion. Further, where an existential conceptualisation of religion is brought together in religious education with a central educational interest of bringing the child to action in plurality, religious education will be better able to resist essentialising or stereotyping religion and religious lives.

6   Discussion: What Might This Mean Practically?

The question from this point becomes one of how this can be achieved? This is interesting since what it means to live with a religious orientation on life conceptualised in existential terms, and not only in relation to beliefs and practices, is not open to study through reason alone. The task or responsibility of the religious education teacher therefore is to find a way to be as a teacher, to teach, in the classroom that is congruent with what religious education should achieve (for further discussion see Biesta & Hannam, 2016; Hannam, 2018). It is at this point then that I return to Weil (especially Weil, 1965) and show how she offers a great deal practically to religious education in the way she writes about 'attention.' Attention is something that is necessary, in a way a pre-requirement, to being able to do anything we might wish to do. Weil's view is that this is especially necessary for academic success (see Weil, 1965, p.69), making it possible for example for the student to see errors in thinking or other matters their teacher might point out. Indeed, in this way the cultivation of attention leads to another valuable quality and this is one of humility or open-mindedness. Nevertheless, to stay for a while longer with attention, I want to make it clear as Weil does (see Weil, 1965, p. 70) that attention cannot be equated with a kind of muscular effort. For Weil, the teacher seeking to bring the child to attend will resemble something like interesting the child in what is to be explored together. But this is not something cognitive exactly, since attention "consists of suspending our thought" (Weil, 1965, p. 72) while at once in some way holding in our mind other things, we may be looking to make connections with. This she says is rather like the way in which someone "who is on a mountain can all at once, see below ... without actually looking at them, a great many forests and plains" (Weil, 1965, p. 72).

The key issue is that if religion is persistently and only brought to the classroom as being something about beliefs in propositional terms or traditions, it is unlikely that the child or young person will be able to 'see' everything all at once in the Weil envisages. The bigger picture for themselves alone and for themselves in relation to all humanity may never come into view. The danger instead is of the objectification, essentialising and stereotyping of religion and those living a religious life, and worse. In addition, as mentioned earlier in this chapter religion only treated as phenomena also tends to divert away from

educational concerns. If instead religious concerns of existence are brought
to the classroom, and in subjective terms, something else altogether may be
possible. This is precisely because bringing the existential into the classroom
necessitates inclusion of the subjective, making it possible to recognise the
importance of recognizing the singularity of the 'I.' I would indeed go on to say
that the attentiveness of which Weil speaks, and which requires the teacher's
recognition of each child, is essential before the child can bring themselves
into study in an intellectually open-minded way. Attention is something the
teacher has a responsibility to call from the child, but perhaps she must also
first call it from herself. Since this is not a transaction between the teacher and
the child, because attention is not something to be paid or given, it is only possible in light of the relationship the teacher has with the child. This is a kind of
relationship where the singularity of the 'I' of both teacher and child are held
dear.

It just remains for me to bring together explicitly the existential conceptualisation of what it means to live a religious life together with Arendt on action
in plurality (see, especially, Arendt, 1958), and for what comes to the surface
from this to be made clear. I have already shown how religious education, is
an opportunity in school life where young people's subjective 'I' can flourish
(see also Biesta chapter 1 in this volume). However, this takes on a new and
critical significance when looked at through the lens of Arendt's insistence on
the importance of our being able to "disclose the 'who'" (Arendt, 1998, p. 180)
of who we are. She makes clear for us that where "speech becomes 'mere talk,'
simply one more means towards the end" (Arendt, 1998, p. 180), the child is
reduced to the point where their humanity is obscured. They are reduced to a
producer (Hannam, 2018 p. 143) and their activity in school reduced to work.
The teacher also risks being reduced to a 'deliverer of curriculum' or a 'facilita-
tor of children's understanding of knowledge.' Action, on the other hand, is
only possible under the condition of plurality and as such is also fragile; it is
never possible in isolation. If what takes place in schools is reduced to mere
fabrication or production by individuals, that is to labour or to work, action in
plurality is not possible and the public sphere is at risk of disappearing. And, as
Arendt explores in much of her work, this is how it is possible for totalitarianism to emerge.

7   Concluding Comments and Future Questions to Be Considered

Religious education's contribution to education is the capacity it has for bringing into the classroom the existential in an explicit way. In so doing religious
education has a particular opportunity for making it possible for each unique

child to be present in the classroom. Religious education's subject-specific responsibility therefore to education lies in the unique interest that religion lived in existential terms has to say about the humanity of each child. This is as someone 'who' (and not as an objective 'what') is coming newly and uniquely into the world. This has implications for religious education in practical terms and especially for the teacher of religious education. For the teacher the implications are both as they consider how they teach as well as the way in which they make choices about a course of study for their children and young people. If the teacher's role is to bring the child to action, through attentiveness and intellectual humility, how can this be achieved?

In addition to exploring faith in her writings, Weil reflects on school and what it is that the teacher can do to cultivate qualities in the child that are needed in order to be prepared, as it were, for education. Weil gives emphasis on the quality of 'attention' making also a clear distinction between 'concentration' or another kind of thing she calls 'will power.' Being attentive is not the same as concentrating 'hard' neither is it the kind of thing that can be willed, neither is it thinking at all. "Attention." says Weil, "consists of suspending our thought ... waiting, ... ready to receive ..." (Weil, 1965, p. 72). Further, 'attention' is not the kind of thing that anyone of us, including teachers, can make or force another to do or to 'pay.'

What is at stake here is the humanity of each child and even of the world itself. There is therefore something vital in this quality of attentiveness. So, as the teacher begins in the classroom, she can begin first by bringing the children to attend to the voices and experience of others in the class. Once a quality of attentiveness becomes familiar, there emerges in the child a kind of intellectual humility where becoming aware of new things in a new kind of way is possible. Again, I don't think this is particularly new or original. It is something perhaps very familiar to the early year's teacher. However, in our day-to-day life with older children too often something that is forgotten. Nevertheless, it is one thing among others that as teachers we need to rediscover, as Biesta (2017) so well explains. The teacher, herself recognising the unique 'who' of each child and young person and throwing open the invitation to attend, is critical for the possibility of the world today and tomorrow.

It is this quality of attention, that can be a starting point for action in plurality. It is attention not only to the material for consideration in the classroom in an intellectually open-minded way, but first to the others present which is what is required in order to bring children and young people to action in plurality. Attentiveness is the prerequisite for each child or young person to be able to discern what is of value for them, and for the world. In this chapter it is proposed that religious education has a very particular thing to achieve by way of contribution to education in the public sphere. Religious education, because (after Weil) of its capacity to recognise the unique 'who,' is where children and young people have the chance to consider and discern, with others, how to exist together in the world. Importantly however, this is discernment not *only* regarding how *I* should live. Rather and precisely because none of us live alone in this world, it is only through risking being drawn into relationship can I begin attend to what others are asking of me and come to action in plurality. And this, as Arendt says, is the miracle that makes the public sphere possible and even that which can save the world.

Note

1   See Home Office publication: *Hate Crime. 2018–2019.* https://assets.publishing.service.gov.uk/government/uploads/system/uploads/attachment_data/file/839172/hate-crime-1819-hosb2419.pdf

References

All Party Parliamentary Group on Religious Education. (2013). *RE: The truth unmasked: The supply and support for religious education teachers.* Religious Education Council of England and Wales.

Arendt, H. (1958). *The human condition.* University of Chicago Press.

Arendt, H. (1961). *Between past and future: Eight exercises in political thought.* Penguin Books.

Arendt, H. (2004). *The origins of totalitarianism.* Schocken Books.

Arweck, E., & Jackson, R. (2012). Religion in education: Findings from the religion and society programme. *Journal of Beliefs & Values, 33*(3), 253–259.

Baumfield, V., & Cush, D. (2013). Religious education at the crossroads (again): The search for a subject identity? *British Journal of Religious Education, (35)*3, 231–253.

Baumfield, V., Cush, D., & Miller, J. (2014). A third perspective in retrospective: 20 years later. *British Journal of Religious Education, 36*(3), 247–255.

Berglund, J., Shanneik, Y., & Bocking, B. (2016). Introduction. In J. Berglund, Y. Shanneik, & B. Bocking (Eds.), *Religious education in a global-local world* (pp. 1–10). Springer.

Biesta, G. (2017). *The rediscovery of teaching.* Routledge.

Chater, M., & Castelli, M. (Eds.). (2017). *We need to talk about religious education: Manifestos for the future of RE.* Jessica Kingsley Publishers.

Clarke, C., & Woodhead, L. (2015). *A new settlement: Religion and belief in schools.* Westminster Faith Debates.

Conroy, J., Lundie, D., Davis, R., Baumfield, V., Barnes, P., Gallagher, T., Lowden, K., Bourque, N., & Wenell, J. (Eds.). (2013). *Does religious education work?* Bloomsbury.

Council of Europe. (2008). Recommendation CM/Rec(2008)12 of the Committee of Ministers to member states on the dimension of religions and non-religious convictions within intercultural education (adopted by the Committee of Ministers on 10 December 2008 at the 1044th meeting of the Ministers' Deputies).

Davis, D., & Miroshnikova, E. (Eds.). (2013). *The Routledge international handbook of religious education.* Routledge.

Dinham, A., & Shaw, M. (2015). *RE for real: The future of teaching and learning about religion and belief.* Goldsmiths.

Gearon, L. (2013). *MasterClass in religious education: Transforming teaching and learning.* Bloomsbury.

Hannam, P. (2018). *Religious education and the public sphere.* Routledge.

Jackson, R. (2011). The interpretive approach as a research tool: Inside the REDCo project. *British Journal of Religious Education, 33*(2), 189–208.

Jackson, R. (2014). The European dimension: Perspectives on religious education from European institutions, professional organisations and research networks. In M. Rothgangel, R. Jackson, & M. Jäggle (in cooperation with P. Klutz & M. Solymar (Eds.), *Religious education at schools in Europe* (pp. 19–41). Vienna University Press/ V&R unipress.

Jackson, R. (2016). Inclusive study of religions and world views in schools: Signposts from the Council of Europe. *Social Inclusion, 4*(2), 14–25.

OSCE/ODHIR. (2007). *Toledo guiding principles on teaching about religions and beliefs in public schools.* OSCE/ODHIR.

Schreiner, P. (2013). Religious education in the European context. *Hungarian Educational Research Journal, 3*(4), 4–14.

Weil, S. (1965). *Waiting for God.* Fontana Books.

Weisse, W. (2010). REDCo: A European research project on religion in education. *Religion & Education, 37*(3), 187–202.

CHAPTER 10

Reflections on the Seminar on *Religion and Education: The Forgotten Dimensions of Religious Education*

Joyce Miller

Abstract

This chapter reflects on the key conference themes of education, religion and religious education. It argues that RE is heading towards crisis and that radical changes must be made. A renewed vision for the subject is required that will encompass religion and worldviews and provide a holistic, objective and inclusive approach for all young people. Biesta's concept of 'subjectification' is endorsed and it is argued that a new pedagogy of relationality – with the 'other,' the 'other-than human' and the 'more-than-human' – can provide the theoretical basis for the exploration of religion, secularity, spirituality and worldviews.

Keywords

objectivity – pedagogy – relationality – religion and worldviews – subjectification

1 Introduction

For two years from September 2016, I had the privilege and responsibility of being a member of the Commission on Religious Education (CoRE), established by but independent of the Religious Education of England and Wales (REC).[1] In the first year, in addition to our central Commission meetings, we travelled around England gathering evidence at five regional events.[2] I also accepted as many invitations as I could from schools, SACRES,[3] and RE organisations to attend meetings and conferences: to speak and to listen, to challenge and be challenged, to think and to question. When, therefore, an invitation was extended for a Commissioner to attend the 'Religion and Education: The Forgotten Dimensions of Religious Education' seminar at Brunel University,

London, in October 2017, I was very keen to participate and to share the insights it offered to my fellow Commissioners. My report on the seminar took the form of presenting the many questions that arose for me on the three areas around which the seminar was structured: education, religion and religious education (RE), and this chapter is an attempt to develop my reflections on those questions further. I do not see my purpose in this volume as providing a summary of the speakers' papers or a critique of the seminar as a whole but rather to offer a retrospective set of thoughts, particularly in light of the debates that have occurred in the two years since the seminar took place.

2   Education

A great deal of my professional work in the last forty years has been with teachers, in initial teacher education and their continuing professional development. One key question to which we returned time and again was the nature and purpose of religious education in schools, especially in regard to maintained schools. It always seemed essential to articulate a philosophy of our subject that was educational and objective. I now feel that while this remains necessary it is not sufficient. What is now needed is a holistic philosophy of education in which religious education (or religion and worldviews, the name for the subject suggestion by the Commission) plays an integral part. For too long, a great deal of RE has been inward focussed, isolated from the rest of the curriculum because of the compromise of the 1988 Education Reform Act which placed it in the basic curriculum and therefore separate from the National Curriculum that dominated the rest of school life. One of the most important lessons we learned on the Commission is that there is very high quality, inspiring RE taking place across the country. We also received damning evidence of lack of support and falling examination entries within an out-dated legal and political framework. A number of high-profile reports had already shown that RE is facing an existential crisis (for example, APPG, 2013; Clarke & Woodhead, 2015, 2018; Conroy et al., 2013; CORAB, 2015; Dinham & Shaw, 2015; NATRE, 2017, 2019; Ofsted, 2007, 2010, 2013). It is now time for radical change and one of those changes lies in the ways in which we think of our subject in the context of schools as a whole: what we can learn and what we can contribute.

   Gert Biesta's three-dimensional approach to education provides the basis on which these professional conversations can be conducted. He proposes three areas into which our work can be divided: qualification, socialisation and subjectification, and the balance between them. His phrase of 'the education imaginary' is pertinent here (Biesta, 2017, p. 44). The importance of 'qualification' and its part in preparing young people for their role in a neoliberal economy has dominated the life of schools for many years now. Of course, teachers have a responsibility to help young people to gain qualifications and to help prepare them for future employment but the domination of this one dimension of education, with its focus on targets and attainment, has been destructive of creativity, professional autonomy, morale and the mental health of both teachers and their students. Many teachers of religious education have greater enthusiasm for Biesta's 'socialisation' and believe that they can make a considerable impact on young people's spiritual, moral, social and cultural development (SMSC). They are supported in this by major work from the Council of Europe which recognises the crucial important of the religious dimension of intercultural education and its benefits for liberal democratic societies (see, for example, Jackson & O'Grady, 2018; Ruth Heilbronn, Chapter 2, this volume). I worry though that RE arrogates too much of the responsibility for SMSC: it is, after all, a cross-curricular responsibility and the whole school ethos must support it. But it is the last of Gert's dimensions that deserves most attention: 'subjectification' and what we mean by that and how it impacts on RE. It is of crucial importance for us, not least because it is the means by which we can address the old question of proselytisation and formation. If education is about 'freedom' then we need to recalibrate our thinking and be able to articulate what this means in relation to RE. By defining subjectification as the freedom to become – "grown up freedom ... when we try to exist in and with the world and not just with ourselves" (Biesta, 2017, p. 98) – Gert enables us to see that we have to be diligent in focussing on learning objectives and not on prescribed outcomes. The etymological connection between 'objectives' and 'objectivity' is important here.

   Since the publication of the 'game-changing' Working Paper 36 (Schools Council, 1971), RE teachers have had to engage with the question of objectivity in relation to subject content which, to use CORE's terminology, has to be 'objective, critical and plural,' all of which terms we need to explore much more deeply as a profession. It's not sufficient to reject 'we' and replace it with 'they' or 'some' or 'most'; it is not sufficient to present a balance of evidence, opinion and belief. There is a need, rather, for teachers to be critically self-reflexive and objective about their own subjectivity: their beliefs, values, opinions and practices, and the ways in which they impact on their selection and presentation of subject content. It is only when we truly respect the subjectivity of our pupils that we will be able to offer a religious education that is inclusive, relevant and thought-provoking for all students, whatever their backgrounds and experiences.

The balance between Gert's three dimensions of education is one that should be at the forefront of professional debate and engagement in our schools, and if discussion of the core purposes and nature of education is not taking place in staffrooms (and worse still, if staffrooms have disappeared) then it's time for teachers to challenge their managers and governors. We are a profession and we have to make reasonable and reasoned professional demands.

3   Religion

It is self-evidently true that the context in which we teach RE today is very different from the context of the 1944 Education Act and the 1988 Education Reform Act. As I found Gert's terminology of the 'educational imaginary' helpful, so too is Charles Taylor's term: 'social imaginary' (Taylor, 2003). Our current social imaginary combines a dominant secularism with deep historical, social and ethical roots in Christianity. Poulat's term 'Christianitude' (quoted by Hervieu-Lèger, 2001, p. 122) is a useful neologism. There is an apparent increasing antipathy to 'religion' and the word itself has become problematic – 'the 'R' word' (Bellah, 2018) – and blamed for a range of social ills from terrorism to misogyny to sexual abuse. There is also a plethora of evidence on declining religious observance and religion as a key self-identifier and yet the 'real religious landscape' (Dinham & Shaw, 2015) is much more complex than statistics would suggest with some religious groups growing, others diminishing in size and new religiosities developing. The complex relationship between religion, worldviews and spirituality requires further study.

A number of papers at the seminar, by Denise Cush and Farid Panjwani, for example,[4] explored the complexities of the terms we use but definitional issues, legal and educational, of both 'religion' and 'worldviews' remain to be addressed further. There is also a need to differentiate more carefully between 'religion' and 'religions,' not least because religious education has tended to use the six main religions (and Humanism) as its subject content, confusing the singular and plural versions of the word. 'Six religions' is not the totality of 'religion.' One of the many great dangers of designing a curriculum around the main six religions is that, by law in England and Wales, the teaching of Christianity has to predominate whilst 'taking account of the *other* religions represented here' (my emphasis). There is a very significant danger here of '*othering*' religions and worldviews that are not Christian and yet, under Human Rights Law, we are required to be 'objective, critical and plural' in both our curriculum design and in classroom practice. These two legal requirements sit very uncomfortably together. Readers of the Commission's recommendations will note that we do not advocate continuing to give precedence to Christianity in our National Entitlement. This is a long-term approach but, in the meantime, avoiding Abrahamic structures in the curriculum and in classroom resources is one way in which teachers can begin to move away from this now out-dated approach (as Denise Cush argues in this volume). Of course, the teaching of Christianity will be highly significant in religious education but there is a need for a new way of thinking about our subject in terms of both content and methodology which will be set out briefly below in the section on religious education.

A further issue remains in relation to 'religion' and that is using religion as the primary or the singular identifier in relation to our fellow human beings. It is a sad fact that since the terrorist attacks of 2001, 'religion' and in particular Islam has become *the* focus of the labels that are attached to people. In some respects, this is understandable because many people choose their religion as their most important form of identity, but this carries dangers (Sen, 2006) and vast oversimplifications (Appiah, 2019). A singular identity becomes immediately exclusionary and offers religion as a focus for negative stereotyping and discrimination. One of the dangers of a systematic approach to the study of religions as separate entities is that their adherents are viewed primarily, or only, as Muslim or Jew or Sikh, and not as fellow human beings searching for meaning to life and answers to fundamental questions about how to live. Religious educators have more work to do on this if we are not, inadvertently, to contribute to reductionist and essentialist views of other people, their religion and their worldviews. David Lewin's chapter in this volume helps us think through this question.

The Commission's understanding of religion and worldviews is that they are both institutional (that is, organised worldviews shared among groups/institutions) *and* that they are personal (an individual's own way of understanding and being in the world). Worldviews – both religious and non-religious – are not just propositional (and here there is close agreement with Patricia Hannam's understanding of religion). Worldviews are not a 'finished product,' as Farid Panjwani points out in Chapter 6 (this volume). They are not fixed and bounded but fluid and dynamic, they are interdependent and interconnected, with fuzzy boundaries, and their patterns of belief, expression and belonging may change. In brief, from the Commission's perspective, worldviews are complex, diverse and plural.

The relationship between individual and institutional worldviews is complex: some people draw on more than one tradition and patterns of belief and belonging may change. The study of religion and worldviews must therefore be pluralist, multi-disciplinary and multi-dimensional (Smart, 1989), as well as objective and critical. This presents huge challenges to teachers of RE who have the difficult task of making religion and worldviews as an area of study accessible, challenging and relevant to their pupils whilst avoiding reductionism and reification.

4   Religious Education

There is need now for a new spatial metaphor for our objective study of religion and worldviews. In the past, we have tended to look forward, horizontally, at the six main religions and Humanism. What we need to do (as well) is to look down and develop an overview of the vastly complex picture of religion and spirituality in the context of secularity, non-belief and commitment. This is our subject content and young people need to understand all these key concepts, the overarching structures of 'religion,' 'secularity,' 'spirituality' and 'worldview.' The spirit in which they will be explored should be one of 'epistemological modesty' for both teachers and pupils: individual principles and commitments will be respected alongside a willingness to learn, to think and to be self-reflexive. As Working Paper 36 declared, nearly 50 years ago, we need 'objectivity about subjectivity'; not just other people's but our own. Our study of religion and worldviews will be characterised by 'methodological agnosticism' so that the acquisition of knowledge and understanding will be gained through a process that has critical engagement at its core. But it is important here to note Bob Bowie's warning in this volume that the binary and conflictual nature of school examination-style religious studies is seen as normative when it is not. Such an approach is inimical to an understanding of the real nature of religion and worldviews and serves only to deepen stereotyping and division.

Patricia Hannam's seminar paper and her subsequent publications (e.g., Hannam, 2018) suggest a three-fold definition of religion: propositional, traditional and existential – that is, religion understood 'existentially as faith.' RE has tended to focus (as has the social imaginary) on the first and second, to the detriment of the third even though it is clear that for people whose key interpretation of life is rooted in religion, the experiential is, almost literally, at its heart. Is 'existential' in Pat's chapter the same as or different from 'experiential'? How can 'faith' be understood by a child who would deny personal experience of the transcendent? How can it be taught without moving into a form of indoctrination or the use of inappropriate teaching methods? My fear is that many RE teachers believe that they have overcome this issue and yet there are times when I find evidence of it. Take, for example, the deployment of meditation as a teaching method in helping pupils to understand

Buddhism, sometimes in the classroom and sometimes on a visit to a Buddhist community. This would seem to be the approach advocated by Have-a-go-Henry in the RE-searchers approach to RE.[5] Meditation and mindfulness practice, although now secularised, have their origins in religious practice (see, for example, Gunther Brown, 2019). This means that pupils are carrying out a religious practice that is probably not their own and one to which their parents might well (and rightly) object. Further, most practitioners of meditation would report that it is a difficult practice. To sit still and breathe for a few minutes and imagine that that is a realistic 'experience' of meditation does not do justice to the complexity and discipline that it in fact requires and the practice is therefore diminished. I assume (and hope) that most teachers in community schools would not ask pupils to pray as part of a RE lesson and yet it is seen as acceptable to ask children to meditate. It isn't. How then to enable pupils to grasp something of the 'experiential'? And how to do this in schools that are, by law, required to promote pupils' spiritual development? The lines become very blurred here and teachers need to tread very careful paths through what is a spiritual minefield, and could, in the most extreme circumstances, become a legal minefield if challenged in the courts. RE teachers are fond of saying that they raise questions rather than offer answers and this is an instance when this writer is tempted to resort to that defence.

And yet, there is a way through this, and it is to rethink our view of pupils' learning and the nature of what it is to be human. We need to see pupils as holistic learners and to recognise that pitting pupils' affective development against cognitive development (learning from and learning about) is an inappropriate binary that we must reject both educationally and philosophically.

For too long, there has been a false dichotomy, particularly in the western world, between body and mind and between mind and heart. When we replace them with a holistic view of ourselves and our pupils as 'whole' then some of the difficulties begin to dissipate. Real learning is always about change; real learning is always transformatory, not just of understanding but of being. As Annie Dillard wrote: "Why are we reading if not in hope of beauty laid bare, life heightened, and its deepest mystery probed?" (Dillard, 2016, p. 111). The nature of our subject matter, exploring the deepest questions of humanity – of existence, in Pat's terminology – will result in reflection and awareness and empathy if teachers provide the ethos and the time for pupils to engage meaningfully and empathetically with their learning. We should demand no less of school structures if we are to fulfil our professional duties appropriately. Schools play a pivotal role in their pupils' 'formation' (Clarke & Woodhead, 2015, p. 33); schools' managers and teachers have to articulate the nature of the formation that they offer and be constantly self-critical and evaluative in what they intend. This particularly important in religious education where the relationship between learning and formation needs to be fully and frequently revisited and carefully analysed.

Gert Biesta has provided in this volume and elsewhere (e.g., Biesta, 2017) the philosophical basis for this: to bring the child into being, "from our being-with-ourselves … [to] being-in-the-world as subject" (Biesta, 2017, p. 83). The freedom to 'become' is not about individualism but about relationality and herein lies the possibility of a pedagogy for our subject of religion and worldviews: a pedagogy of relationality. This will see the child coming to 'grown-up-ness' (Biesta, 2017, p. 16) in relation to the 'other,' to the 'other-than-human' (Berry, 1999) and to the 'more-than-human' (Reason, 2017). By 'other' I understand our fellow human beings, all of whom are different from us and with whom we must learn to live without violence and in collaboration. By the 'other-than-human' I understand the whole of the natural world and there is a developing ecological spirituality from which religion and worldviews, as a subject, can draw. By the 'more-than-human' I understand the experiences of depth and transcendence, for both spatial metaphors can offer a means of articulating spirituality. Thus, a pedagogy of relationality would provide a theoretical foundation for the spiritual, moral, social, cultural and cognitive development of the child – as an independent, free, holistic being – in relation to religion and worldviews.

5   Conclusion

My reactions to and reflections on the Brunel seminar have changed in the two years since the event took place as I have read, talked and listened more on the nature and purpose of what we have called religious education for at least the last thirty years. The seminar has helped me to conclude that we need radical change and I believe the Commission on RE's final report sets out the direction that change needs to take. The views of 'religion' presented in the seminar are in keeping with many of these changes. We have understood the term too narrowly in the past to give it real relevance for the majority of young people in our schools who do not align themselves with a single religious worldview. Linda Rudge's article (1998) identified the need for those who would describe themselves as 'nothing' but their needs have not yet been addressed, thirty years on. We now need to be more inclusive and to broaden and deepen our subject content to explore religion *and* worldviews. That must, of course, include what Pat calls 'the existential,' that is, to do with our existence, and yet do so in a way that never aims to move beyond the 'participant observer' role into the 'participant' only.

Above all, pupils have to be seen holistically and teachers' key responsibility for their development is one of nurturing their growth and independence, emphasising their coming to freedom in the context of 'the other'. This must be defined in very broad terms to include not just other people who are different from them (though that is essential) but the fragile earth we inhabit and the possibility of the 'other' as ineffable.

Notes

1   Our final report, CoRE (2018) *Religion and worldviews: The way forward. A national plan for RE* is available at https://www.commissiononre.org.uk/wp-content/uploads/2018/09/Final-Report-of-the-Commission-on-RE.pdf
2   The Commission's remit covered England only.
3   SACREs are Standing Advisory Council on Religious Education. Every Local Authority in England and Wales must have one, its membership categories determined by statute, with a duty to support and monitor religious education and collective worship. One of their duties is to establish a Conference for quinquennial review of the locally Agreed Syllabus for RE. This is known as local determination and stands in relation to but not part of the National Curriculum.
4   Professor Denise Cush and Professor Farid Panjwani were both members of CoRE.
5   https://www.reonline.org.uk/re-searchers-approach/the-characters/

References

Appiah, K. A. (2019). *The lies that bind.* Profile Books.
APPG (All Party Parliamentary Group on RE). (2013). *The truth unmasked.* Retrieved November 4, 2019, from https://www.religiouseducationcouncil.org.uk/resources/documents/religious-education-the-truth-unmasked/
Bellah, R. (2018). The 'R' word. *Tricycle*, Spring. Retrieved November 4, 2019, from https://tricycle.org/magazine/the-r-word/
Biesta, G. J. J. (2017). *The rediscovery of teaching.* Routledge.
Berry, T. (1999). *The great work.* Three Rivers Press.
Clarke, C., & Woodhead, L. (2015). *A new settlement: Religion and belief in schools.* Westminster Faith Debates.
Clarke, C., & Woodhead, L. (2018). *A new settlement revised: Religion and belief in schools.* Westminster Faith Debates.
Conroy, J., Lundie, D., Davis, R., Baumfield, V., Barnes, P., Gallagher, T., Lowden, K., Bourque, N., & Wenell, J. (Eds.). (2013). *Does religious education work?* Bloomsbury.
CORAB (Commission on Religion and Public Life). (2015). *Living with difference.* Retrieved November, 22, 2019, from https://www.woolf.cam.ac.uk/assets/file-downloads/Living-with-Difference.pdf

Dillard, A. (2016). *The abundance.* Canongate.

Dinham, A., & Shaw, M. (2015). *RE for real: The future of teaching and learning about religion and belief.* Goldsmiths.

Gunther Brown, C. (2019). *Debating yoga and mindfulness in public schools.* University of North Carolina Press.

Hannam, P. (2018). *Religious education and the public sphere.* Routledge.

Hervieu-Lèger, D. (2001). The two-fold limit of the notion of secularization. In L. Woodhead, P. Heelas, & D. Martin (Eds.), *Peter Berger and the study of religion* (pp. 112–125). Routledge.

Jackson, R., & O'Grady, K. (2018). The religious and worldview dimension of intercultural education: The Council of Europe's contribution. *Intercultural Education, 30*(3), 247–259.

NATRE. (2016). *The State of the Nation.* NATRE and REC. Retrieved 22 November, 2019, from https://www.religiouseducationcouncil.org.uk/wp-content/uploads/2017/07/State-of-the-Nation-Report-2017.pdf

NATRE. (2019). *An analysis of a survey of teachers on the impact of government policy on student opportunity to study GCSE RS.* Religious Education Council of England and Wales & National Association of Teachers of RE.

Ofsted. (2007). *Making sense of religion.* Author.

Ofsted. (2010). *Transforming religious education.* Author.

Ofsted. (2013). *Religious Education: Realising the potential.* Author.

Reason, P. (2017). *In search of grace: An ecological pilgrimage.* Earth Books.

Rudge, L. (1998). I am nothing'–does it matter? A critique of current religious education policy and practice in England on behalf of the silent majority. *British Journal of Religious Education, 20*(3), 155–165.

Schools Council. (1971). *Working paper 36 Religious education in secondary schools.* Methuen Educational.

Sen, A. (2006). *Identity and violence.* Allen Lane.

Smart, N. (1989). *The world's religions.* Cambridge University Press.

Taylor, C. (2003). *Modern social imaginaries.* Duke University Press.

Reflecting on the Forgotten Dimensions of Religious Education: Conclusions and Ways Forward

Patricia Hannam and Gert Biesta

Abstract

This chapter offers an analysis of some common themes that have emerged through the essays in the book and which seem likely to merit further research. Each of the essays were written in response to questions in relation to the constituent elements of the subject: education and religion. Although there is scope for further research regarding religion, it has become clear there is urgent need for greater interrogation of educational theory underpinning religious education. Without analysis of the educational underpinning of religious education, the significant contribution religion has to bring to education in the public sphere, seems likely to be missed.

Keywords

education – subjectification – socialisation – essentialism – text – hermeneutics – action

1 Introduction

As we write the closing words of this book a large part of the world's population is staying home, due to the coronavirus pandemic. Schools across Europe have been closed for weeks to all but essential workers' children and the most vulnerable. Children, young people and their parents as well as teachers and policy makers, in many different national contexts, have an unexpected opportunity to see what education might mean for them, their communities and our shared world, in a new way. This situation is not just for a few days or weeks, like a school holiday, but for months. Tens of thousands of people have died around the world and the number sadly is certain to have risen further by the time this book is published. The future is uncertain. If we were not already in an 'existential crisis,' as Greta Thunberg (2019) has warned us, for sure we are each face to face with our own mortality now. Little did we know how timely some of the thinking in this book might turn out to be.

This closing chapter intends to discern some of the insights that have come into view through the chapters presented here. Each chapter has sought to respond to fundamental questions about the role, status and position of religion and education in religious education and here a conversation is begun around some of the key points arising.

Discussions about what religious education in schools *is* and what it should be *for* have been going on for many years in many countries around the world. Such discussions have resulted in an array of viewpoints and practical materials for curricula and teaching practices, however little time has till now been taken to reflect on the constituent elements of the subject, religion and education. Each of the chapters in this book, in a different way, has quite explicitly explored fundamental questions which have in a sense been forgotten in the field of religious education. Biesta, Heilbronn and Aldridge have focused on the question of education in relation to religious education, while Cush and Robinson and Lewin have shed new light on religion itself. Biesta's interview with Panjwani and Revell has revealed some of the problems of essentialising religion, and links with themes that emerged from Cush's and Robinson's chapter. Whittle has undertaken a focussed consideration of the place of theology in religious education, focusing particularly on Catholic religious education, whilst Bowie has provided an exploration of the problems this has led to in public examinations. All of this raises once more, but in new ways, the ever-pressing question of how religion should be (re)presented in the classroom. Biesta's and Hannam's chapters bring much of this together and offer new possibilities for religious education. In what follows we discuss some of the emerging themes and provide suggestions of areas which we consider likely to benefit from further, and indeed perhaps urgent, research.

We encourage the reader to approach this book with an open mind so as to allow for the possibility that religious education is not only about what we want children and young people to know, but also about what we hope they will be able to do with what they know. This is not only because education is more complex than knowing things in terms of remembering them and being able to reproduce them, but also because what it means to live a religious life is not one thing either (see Cush and Robinson, Whittle, and Hannam). Therefore, a religious education concerned with taking the subject-ness of the student seriously (see Biesta), will need to look beyond religion as an object of study and has to take the existential dimension of religion seriously (see Whittle and

Hannam). This in turn will mean that religious education as a school subject has some very particular responsibilities (see for example Biesta, Aldridge and Hannam) and has to be concerned directly with how young people discern how they live their lives. Religious education as an educational opportunity for discernment will change what it is that the teacher should understand herself as doing. Further it will lead to a considerable transformation of curriculum and public examinations. Perhaps this kind of religious education is one that the world needs right now. Another world is possible, one in which religious education must step up to what is required at this time.

2   Education: The Most Forgotten Dimension of Religious Education?

Education has perhaps been the most forgotten dimension of religious education. It is therefore fitting that this book has begun with chapters that give consideration to some broader questions in relation to education and to what it should seek to achieve. Biesta, in Chapter 1, discusses three purposes or domains of educational purpose: qualification, socialisation and subjectification. He suggests these are like a 'threefold educational prism' by which we can not only see better what is wrong with more one-sided conceptions of education, but also how this should also be of utmost importance in research, policy and practice. Biesta raises the question of freedom in relation to education, something that Hannam picks up on this point later in Chapter 9, as well discussing freedom in more depth particularly in relation to religious education (see Hannam, 2018).

Heilbronn, in Chapter 2, takes a different track in discussing education as a social practice, bringing the work of John Dewey into the discussion. Heilbronn's chapter links strongly with Biesta's consideration of the socialisation dimension of education and in so doing opens up new ways of considering religious education. Aldridge picks up the educational discussion in Chapter 3, emphasising the significance of an "existential relationship between teacher, student and their shared object of study." He is concerned to give a descriptive account of what he terms as an 'existential possibility' present within all education. In the closing paragraphs of his chapter he considers the implications of this proposal for the curriculum subject religious education.

Both Aldridge and Heilbronn raise the significance of dialogue in educational contexts. Heilbronn, drawing on Dewey and Aldridge going to philosophical hermeneutics, in particular the work of Gadamer and Heidegger. Whilst Aldridge and Heilbronn both emphasise the relational nature of education, Aldridge emphasises a three-way relationship between the teacher, the student and the material being engaged with, setting out what he terms a 'pedagogy of belonging.' However, although relationship is clearly important, it is Biesta who brings our attention not only to the relationship, but also to the significance of asking the question 'who' is in that relationship. He emphasises that education has a greater responsibility than only the 'cultivation of an object' but should take interest in the subjectification of each child as one 'called into existence' in the world.

Hannam, in Chapter 9, also contributes to the discussion regarding what it is that education should seek to achieve. She emphasises the significance of the relationships between those in the classroom, using insights from Hannah Arendt, building an argument for education being understood as bringing the child to 'action in plurality.' She goes further to explain how this might happen in relation first to bringing the child to attend. The difference between this and Aldridge's three-way relationship is perhaps subtle and qualitative, in that attentiveness is a quality that becomes possible under certain conditions and not something the teacher can ensure that the child will give. The relationships between what is being studied, for example a text, the child and the teacher are not the same, since human beings are not objects but subjects of their own lives (see also Biesta, 2017).

The way texts are engaged with in religious education, is also considered by Bowie in Chapter 8 as well as Biesta's interview with Panjwani and Revell in Chapter 6, and in this sense could benefit from being read alongside Aldridge's chapter. Panjwani's and Revell's concern is about essentialising religion in religious education, a concern shared by Bowie and for which they both suggest a hermeneutical approach could help to resolve. Whittle, in Chapter 7, takes up Biesta's analysis of the emphasis on 'teaching and learning' in recent times as discussed briefly in Chapter 1 and also as developed extensively elsewhere (see, for example, Biesta, 2012, 2014, 2017). Whittle draws attention especially to Biesta's point that there has been an unhelpful over-emphasis on learning, which he describes as the problem of 'learnification,' emphasising the importance of reconsidering the significance of teaching in relation to religious education – something Miller also discusses in Chapter 10. This brings us to the consideration of what it is that is brought to the child in religious education and so to the question of what counts as religion, the second forgotten dimension.

3   What Counts as Religion in Religious Education?

The final report of the Commission on RE (CoRE, 2017) raised the possibility of changing the name of the school subject 'Religious Education' to 'Religion and Worldviews,' questioning the subject matter therefore to be included in the school curriculum. The question as to what should constitute the disciplinary edges of religious education is something that has been explored in the wider religious education literature extensively in recent years, and Cush and Robinson open this discussion in their chapter. They begin by distinguishing, firstly, between popular understandings of religion, secondly the way it has been approached in university religious studies departments, and thirdly with adherent's views, however this leads them to question whether the term 'religion' is any longer useful. Cush and Robinson go further, giving a brief but clear account of the way in which 'Western' influences have led to a particular construction of Asian religions, many in the Dharmic tradition. Much of this discussion links well with what Hannam terms different 'conceptualisations' of religions (see also Hannam, 2018).

In Chapter 7, Whittle makes the point that any distinction between faith and theology will turn on the way 'faith' is understood. Whittle, like Hannam, recognises that the concept of faith is rooted in the Greek *pistes*. However, Whittle also identifies the etymological significance of the Latin word *fiducare* and makes the point that that these differing roots have allowed for at least two dominant meanings to emerge. The first characterises faith as a stance of loyalty or commitment to some person or cause whereas the second places emphasis on assenting to a set of beliefs. In addition, this set of beliefs will usually have been identified or specified by others from a position of authority.

Hannam's point here would be that these conceptualisations of religion must be linked carefully with what it is one regards education as seeking to achieve. This is perhaps part of what Bowie is saying with regard to public examinations, where great emphasis is currently placed on students being able to develop 'logical chains of argumentation.' A problem with this is that it forces an interpretation of religion into a place, as Bowie explains, where it is not suited. This is because logical reasoning is not what is at the heart of what it means to live a life of faith.

Biesta's interview with Panjwani and Revell brings to the discussion here an interrogation of problems of what can happen when religion is limited and essentialised in the classroom, especially with regard to the case of teaching Islam. Whereas Panjwani and Revell advocate a hermeneutic approach to teaching in order to resolve these issues, Lewin takes up the problem in a different way. He recognises that the teacher has to make choices, not least because of time constraints, about how to represent religion to children and young people in the classroom. Teachers have to make the material intelligible in the way they present it and they also have to make some selection of what to present. The challenge is how to do that without oversimplification, knowing that there will necessarily be a reduction. At this point there is a strong resonance here with Cush and Robinson's chapter, for both acknowledge the complexity of the broad area of concern we are in when speaking about religion. Cush and Robinson look to widening the field and considering 'worldviews.' However, Lewin suggests we must accept the necessity of the teacher making difficult choices and instead introduces the distinction between reductionism and 'pedagogical reduction.' This move is significant in ensuring that emphasis is placed upon the need for teachers to engage with educational questions in relation to our subject.

4   Is an Educational Religious Education Possible?

It would seem that the chapters in this book show that an educational religious education is possible. However, for this to be the case, religious education needs to be much more securely rooted in educational theory. It is therefore likely that this will be an important area where more work needs to be undertaken, both in terms of theoretical exploration as well as in terms of how this translates into practice. In Chapter 10, Miller reminds us that teachers of religious education must recognise that children and young people in school are coming into the world of others, and that an important educational task of religious education must be to connect with this. Miller looks to Biesta's wider work in opening this important conversation, which Biesta frames in terms of socialisation and subjectification. We hope that readers of this book will find other chapters in this book contribute to their further reflections on this point and that further research is begun.

Where teachers and policy makers position religious education educationally, will have practical implications for syllabus development as well as curriculum formation. It will be important, therefore, for those in position of influence to recognise is the pressing need for research to be undertaken to expose and formulate the educational positioning of religious education. It will of course also be vital to take due consideration for what is regarded as forming the boundaries of the subject, that is to say what counts as religion in religious education. But only taking religion into account is just half of what has to be done. Bowie's discussions in Chapter 8 regarding public examinations, shows clearly why it is important to improve appreciation of this relationship. Hannam and Whittle's problematisation of faith, in this volume and elsewhere (see for example Hannam, 2018), may also reveal additional fruitful areas of research regarding the contribution of religious education to the subjectification domain of education (see also Biesta and Miller).

Cush's and Robinson's chapter, taken together with the exploration of what it means to live a religious life contained in Whittle's and Hannam's chapters, show that there are likely to be qualitatively different characteristics in materials used in the classroom. From Hannam's work with Arendt and Weil, there seem to be some emerging and promising practical developments at classroom level. But in relation to this, another area of pressing research also emerges. Heilbronn and Aldridge both bring our attention to the importance of the relationship between the child and the teacher, and Aldridge introduces the text or materials into the matrix. But are the relationships between these three elements equal? This raises questions not only of responsibility but also of power. Cush and Robinson raise this in relation to colonial interpretations of religion that in some cases prevail in European classrooms, while Hannam raises this in relation to the political and the public sphere.

All this will also have implications for teacher education provision and continuing professional education. Indeed, this was something recognised in the CoRE report (2017). Lewin's chapter shows how important it is for teachers of religious education to be able to make wise choices and selections which do not defer to reductionism or lead to the essentialising of any tradition. There is also further theoretical and practical research to be undertaken in relation to the part philosophical hermeneutics can play in the teaching of religious education, particularly in order to see whether this is a sufficiently educational proposal as Aldridge and Panjwani and Revell propose.

5   Concluding Comments and Areas for Further Research

In bringing together the chapters of this book, we have sought to shed light on the complexities of religious education, specifically with regard to its constituting dimensions, religion and education. Questions around where the educational positioning of the subject lies have too frequently been forgotten. Our interest here has not been to ask why this has happened, or indeed whether it has happened more in religious education than in other subjects or in England more than in other national contexts. In bringing this book together we do not seek to recommend one particular solution over another. Rather we hope that readers in England, the UK, Europe and beyond, will find something here that enables them to gain orientation in the glorious complexity of religious education and to continue the journey through that complexity, rather than to avoid it.

Nevertheless, it does seem that an important first starting point is to clarify what it is education should seek to achieve at this point in history. This does not mean that the subject matter that constitutes religious education is not also important; far from it. However, it does mean that those interested and engaged in religious education, should perhaps take a broader view and in this way find themselves better able to articulate the distinctive contribution religion can offer to education in the public sphere and, significantly, to this point in history.

References

Biesta, G. (2012). Giving teaching back to education. Responding to the disappearance of the teacher. *Phenomenology and Practice, 6*(2), 35–49.

Biesta, G. (2014). *The beautiful risk of education.* Routledge.

Biesta, G. (2017). *The rediscovery of teaching.* Routledge.

Hannam, P. (2018). *Religious education and the public sphere.* Routledge.

Hannam, P., & Biesta, G. (2019). Religious education, a matter of understanding? Reflections on the final report of the commission on religious education. *Journal of Beliefs and Values, 40*(1), 55–63.

CoRE (Commision on Religious Education). (2018). *Religion and worldviews: The way forward. A national plan for RE.* Final report. Religious Education Council of England and Wales. Retrieved April 3, 2020, from https://www.religiouseducationcouncil.org.uk/wp-content/uploads/2017/05/Final-Report-of-the-Commission-on-RE.pdf

Thunberg, G. (2019, September). Speech at the beginning of the UN's Climate Action Summit. Retrieved April 2, 2020, from https://news.un.org/en/story/2019/09/1047052

Index